The Essential

Guide for Helping Refugees

Includes Status Determination, Training and Advocacy

Edited by Patrick Sookhdeo

Contents

Preface

As I write, the nation of Syria is blighted by lawlessness and civil war, and many of its endangered Christians are trying desperately to escape their stricken country. Hundreds of families have put themselves in the hands of human traffickers or endured treacherous journeys to reach Europe. Some have sold all their possessions to pay for their passage, or have almost died en route. Yet when they arrive, they may not be welcome or safe.

This tragic and continuing story highlights the plight of so many Christians around the world who are forced by persecution to become refugees far from home. The challenges they face are immense. Many arrive in other countries with few or no possessions, separated from their families and lacking even basic legal papers. Some are traumatised by their past experiences and fearful of any form of authority. Often they lack the ability to communicate in the language of their host country. They may face immediate deportation or constant harassment by the police. "Home" for some becomes a refugee camp.

Those who have become refugees because they have converted to Christianity face additional grave difficulties, not least when they apply for refugee status.Those who assess their applications may suspect that their conversions are just a means of securing asylum. Even well-meaning non-Christian officials may find such assessments difficult, and inappropriate questions have sometimes been asked in their attempts to get at the truth. Some officers and interpreters may also be hostile to the applicants' decisions to convert and therefore be biased against them. Many applicants are not given an adequate opportunity to present their case.

These factors and others leave Christian refugees extremely vulnerable and in great need of support and guidance from people whom they can trust. Churches are increasingly meeting the needs of Christian (and other) refugee applicants spiritually, physically, and also professionally, by creating groups of lawyers and advisors from within the congregations who are willing to provide assistance during various stages of the refugee application process.

The creation of this manual was inspired by Barnabas Fund's commitment to support the persecuted Church. It is designed to provide practical guidance for our worldwide partners and supporters who want to help Christians who arrive in our communities and are seeking refugee status. It can be used as both a reference tool for those who find themselves supporting a particular individual, and a training resource for groups of volunteers who want to offer their services to fellow-Christians driven by oppression to become refugees.

The manual outlines the basics of international refugee law and the procedures involved in securing refugee status. It also offers recommendations for guiding Christian refugees through this often difficult and challenging process.

When we serve other Christians who are strangers in a land that is not their own, our Lord accepts what we do as service to Him (Matthew 25:35, 40). It is our prayer that this manual will empower Christians, Christian organisations and Christian leaders to support their brothers and sisters in Christ who come among us in such desperate need.

Dr Patrick Sookhdeo
International Director, Barnabas Fund

FOUNDATIONS

THE LEGAL FRAMEWORK THAT GOVERNS REFUGEES

this section, the reader will be introduced to the standards that govern the rights of refugees according to the UN Convention Relating to the Status of Refugees of 1951 (CRSR) (the Convention)[1] and its Additional Protocol of 1967 (the Protocol)[2].

The purpose of this section of the manual is to provide the user with an understanding of the legal framework that determines whether the circumstances of an individual's departure from a country actually meet the legal criteria required for him/her to be considered a refugee.

The first recognition of an international right to seek asylum can be found in the Universal Declaration of Human Rights (UDHR). Article 14.1 states that "everyone has the right to seek and to enjoy in other countries asylum from persecution".[3]

The United Nations Convention Relating to the Status of Refugees (CRSR) is an international convention that has been ratified by the majority of states that represent the international community.

The convention represents the main legal instrument concerning refugees. The convention defines who is a refugee and therefore who may qualify for asylum. The convention details the rights of individuals who have been granted asylum and also the responsibilities of states that grant asylum to individuals.

According to Article 1A.2 of the Convention, a refugee is someone who

> *owing to a well-found fear of being persecuted for reasons of race, religion, nationality, membership in a particular social group or political opinion, is outside the country of his nationality and is unable or, owing to such fear, is unwilling to avail himself of the protection of that country; or who, not having a nationality and being outside of the country of his former habitual residence as a result of such events, is unable or, owing to such fear, is unwilling to return to it.*[4]

States that have signed the Convention and its Additional Protocol are responsible for providing protection to refugees. These states are allowed to administer refugee status determination (RSD) themselves as long as they conform to the general standards of the Convention and Protocol.

The Office of the United Nations High Commissioner for Refugees (commonly referred to as the UNHCR) is a United Nations agency that is responsible for the protection and support of refugees at the request of either a government or the UN.

The UNHCR has three core functions: assisting in the voluntary repatriation of refugees, working to effect integration into the local community, and facilitating resettlement of refugees to a third country. In addition the UNHCR has a global governance role of leading and co-ordinating international action to protect refugees and resolving refugee problems worldwide.

The UNHCR has its headquarters in Geneva, Switzerland and has field offices in the countries where it works. The UNHCR has a website (www.unhcr.org) that contains a great deal of useful information concerning its work.

The Convention itself does not set out specific procedures for the determination of refugee status (RSD). In this context the UNHCR may function as an advisor to states that perform RSD. Examples of states that conduct their own RSD process include Australia, Canada, the United States and the member states of the European Union. For states that are not parties to the Convention or Protocol, the UNHCR is responsible for RSD.

The first section of this manual focuses on the procedures and stages involved in RSD when administered by the UNHCR. The second section provides advice and guidance for those individuals, churches or organisations that wish to provide support to individuals who are applying for RSD.

Diagram 1-1 below lists the relevant inquiries required to prove refugee status under the Convention.[5]

Refugee Definition under the Geneva Convention of 1951

What does it mean to be a refugee?

The definition of a refugee under the Convention can be separated into four distinct elements. An individual must be able to show evidence to satisfy the requirements of each element to be legally classified as a refugee.

> The person must have a well-founded fear of persecution for any of the specific listed reasons, namely: race, religion, nationality, political opinions or membership of a particular social group.
>
> [T]he person must be outside the country of his or her nationality or, if stateless, outside the country of his or her formal habitual residence.
>
> [T]he person must be unable or, owing to such fear, unwilling to avail him or herself of the protection of that country.

These elements become the test used by the decision-makers in determining individual applications for RSD. For the applicant to succeed they must show how the facts of their particular experience satisfy the requirements of each of these elements and therefore meets the test.

What sources of guidance exist to provide guidance as to how these elements are interpreted?

1. The UNHCR Handbook on Procedures and Criteria for Determining Refugee Status

The UNHCR's considered interpretation of each of these elements is contained in the UNHCR Handbook on Procedures and Criteria for Determining Refugee Status, which can be accessed on the UNHCR website: www.unhcr.org/ 3d58e13b4.html.

The handbook also serves as an important source of law for countries that are party to the Convention relating to the determining of asylum applications, but state parties are not required to follow the guidance contained in the UNHCR handbook. It does not have the force of law in any country, but it is an authoritative guide to the interpretation of the Convention. It is therefore very useful as a reference tool when assisting individuals who are applying to the UNHCR for refugee status determination.

2. Decided case law of the appellate courts of countries who are party to the Convention

Decisions made by judges from the Appellate Courts of primary resettlement countries[6] (i.e. United States, United Kingdom, Canada and Australia) also play an influential role in developing definitions of the elements. Cases decided by appellate courts in the primary resettlement countries also shape how those countries will interpret refugee status.

These judicial decisions may be binding for resettlement countries but they are not obligatory on other countries including a host country performing RSD, or on the UNHCR. Thus they may provide an argument for a particular interpretation, but local decision-makers are not required to follow the decision of another country's courts.

In this sub-section we consider the basic requirements for each of the four elements that establish refugee status

Owing to a well-founded fear

The well-founded fear element has two components:

i. The applicant must possess a genuine fear of persecution if they were to be returned to their country (the subjective element of fear)

ii. The fear possessed must be well-founded, which means there must be a serious possibility of persecution actually happening if the applicant is returned to their home country

The subjective element of fear

In determining whether the requisite fear exists, the UNHCR considers, among other things:

i. the factual circumstances that led to the applicant deciding to leave his or her country of nationality

ii. the personal and family background of the applicant

iii. their membership of a particular racial, religious, national, social or political group

iv. evidence about how the state or fellow citizens regard that particular racial, religious, national, social or political group

v. the applicant's own interpretation of his situation, and

vi. their personal experiences, including past threats of persecution and incidences of actual persecution in the past

The well-founded fear must focus on the risk of persecution occurring in the future if the applicant is returned to his or her country. More specifically, the feared persecution must be "reasonably possible" in the context of the objective circumstance, which takes us to the second component.[7] The onus is on the applicant to establish that there is a real risk of persecution happening.

The objective determination of whether such fear is "well-founded".

The first component, of subjective fear, is evaluated on a case-by-case basis, but the second, objective component is based upon an investigation into the circumstances that exist in the relevant country.[8] Many decision-makers often refer to annual country survey reports produced by other governments. Human rights reports produced by international organisations should also be referred to.

This objective determination requires the decision-makers within the UNHCR to have an up-to-date understanding of the general human rights record of the applicant's country of origin. This information is then compared to the testimony of the claimant.[9]

Case law related to "well-founded fear"

In Al Najar v. Ashcroft, the 11th Circuit Court of Appeals found that the refugee applicant's fear of persecution must be "subjectively genuine and objectively reasonable".[10] As to the burden of proof related to the objective element, the Supreme Court of the United States in Immigration and Naturalization Service v. Cardozo-Fonseca[11] states, "[T]o show a 'well-founded fear of persecution', an alien need not prove that it is more likely than not that he or she will be persecuted in his or her home country." In regard to well-founded fear, a UK court[12] held that *[t]he requirement that an applicant for refugee status had to have a "well-founded" fear of persecution if he was returned to his own country meant that there had to be demonstrated a reasonable degree of likelihood that he would be so persecuted, and in deciding whether the applicant had made out his claim that his fear of persecution was well-founded the Secretary of State could take into account facts and circumstances known to him or established to his satisfaction but possibly unknown to the applicant in order to determine whether the applicant's fear was objectively justified.*

Persecution

The Convention does not define persecution, nor is there a universally accepted definition of what counts as persecution.

The Convention does makes clear that the persecution feared must be linked to one of the specified grounds under the Convention, namely race, religion, nationality, membership of a particular social group or political opinion. Persecution for another reason will not satisfy the requirements of the definition of a refugee.

The UNHCR has general categories that it has determined to count as persecution. These include:

i. a threat to life and liberty on account of race, religion, nationality, political opinion or membership of a particular social group

ii. discrimination of a substantially prejudicial nature that would, for instance, severely restrict the claimant's ability to work, practise his/her religion or access educational opportunities

iii. discrimination that is not in itself sufficient for persecution but that produces anxiety, apprehension or insecurity regarding a claimant's future existence, and criminal prosecution or fear of it for one of the reasons listed in the definition[13]

iv. serious violations of specific human rights for any of the listed reasons

v. being forced to live in very dire social and economic conditions

Whether other prejudicial actions or threats amount to persecution depends on the circumstances of each case.[14]

In light of these categories, the following are some concrete examples of persecution:

i. Persecution may involve cumulative, specific instances of violence or harassment towards an individual and his or her family members, according to the decision of the US Court of Appeals for the Ninth Circuit in Korablina v. Immigration and Naturalization Services.[15]

ii. Substantial economic discrimination can rise to the level of persecution. Persecution may either be carried out by the state authorities (national, regional or local government, state institutions such as the police or the armed forces) or by individual citizens. If the alleged persecution is carried out by individuals or sections of the population there must also be evidence to show that the state is knowingly tolerating this persecution or that the state is either unable or unwilling to provide effective protection to the targeted individual.

iii. A threat of serious harm can amount to persecution, especially when it causes a person to alter his or her behaviour. The use of the legal system of a country to harass individuals may in certain circumstances amount to persecution: for example, where the state laws prohibit normal human activity that is protected by fundamental human rights, such as by making it a criminal offence to change one's religious beliefs, or to practise a particular religion, or to hold a particular political view.

"[T]he persecution must be for reasons of race, religion, nationality, membership of a particular social group or political opinion"

This requirement means that the persecution must be connected to one or more of the specified grounds listed in the Convention. It is sufficient for this ground to be a relevant factor contributing to the persecution; it need not be an exclusive or dominant cause. The claimant may also cite more than one ground.

There are circumstances in which the claimant does not objectively satisfy any of the grounds, but the claimant may be suffering persecution because persecutors impute such a ground to him.[16]

For instance, an Iraqi Christian may be persecuted because his persecutors believe that he is supportive of the "Christian" conquest of Iraq by American and British soldiers. The Iraqi Christian may be opposed to the US invasion, but his persecutors believe he is complicit with foreign, Christian action.

Race

Race is to be construed broadly to include colour, descent and national or ethnic origin. Frequently race will also entail membership of a specific social group of common descent that forms a minority within a larger population.[17] Examples include individuals of Chinese descent who live and work among ethnic Malays in Malaysia, and Kurds living in Turkey, Iraq or Iran.

The existence of racial discrimination (and distinction, exclusion, restriction or preference based on race, colour, descent or national or ethnic origin) will be an important element in establishing a claim to persecution on the basis of race.

Religion

Examples of religious persecution would include:

- **i.** a total ban on worship or religious instruction
- **ii.** severe discrimination that renders life unbearable against those who profess a particular religious belief
- **iii.** severe state-imposed penalties in certain countries against Muslims who convert to another faith[18]
- **iv.** having to practise religion underground to avoid punishment[19]
- **v.** punishment for proselytism if this is an essential part of the religion's witness

Different courts have addressed the issue of proselytism and persecution in different ways. The issue is whether applicants should not proselytise when they know that to do so would attract persecution. Some cases in which this issue is discussed involve the persecution of members of the Ahmadi sect of Islam in Pakistan.

The most recent case of this kind decided by the English courts is Ahmad (Iftikhar) v Secretary of State for the Home Department [2000] INLR 1. The court determined that a claim for refugee status would not be defeated on the basis that the applicant is inviting persecution by his actions. The decision was influenced by the fact that proselytism is part of the fundamental right of freedom of religion under the UDHR and the International Covenant on Civil and Political Rights.

In Kassatkine v. Canada, the Canadian Federal Court found that a national law in Moldova that prohibited proselytism constituted persecution against evangelical Baptists who engaged in public proselytisation in accordance with the tenets of their belief system.[20] The Court in Kasstkine held:

> *[a] law which requires a minority of citizens to breach the principles of their religion [or] to be lifelong outlaws, is patently persecutory. One might add, so long as those religious tenets are not unreasonable as, for example, exacting human sacrifice or taking of prohibited drugs as a sacrament.*[21]

Definition of religion[22]

Religion in this context involves one or more of the following elements:

i. "Religion as belief" includes theistic, non-theistic and atheistic beliefs. Claimants may be regarded as "heretics, apostates, schismatic, pagans or superstitious, even by other adherents of their religious tradition and be persecuted for that reason."[23] For instance, religion as belief can involve agreement to particular doctrines such as those of the Apostles' Creed or the Nicene Creed.

ii. Religion may be understood as an identity. In this context, religion may be more of a matter of membership in a group bound by common beliefs or traditions rather than a matter of personal theological conviction.[24] For instance, a person may consider himself a Catholic even though he has not been to a Catholic church in twenty years and has little knowledge of the Bible. He may have grown up around Catholic culture and consider himself a Catholic despite having little personal commitment to Catholicism.

iii. Religion may be defined as a "way of life". Religion is understood as involving certain celebrations, wearing distinctive clothes and meeting certain dietary requirements, for example, the requirement for a Jew or a Muslim to avoid eating pork.[25]

Case law related to religious persecution

i. Interference with religious observance can constitute persecution. For instance, the U.S. Court of Appeals for the Seventh Circuit in Kantoni v. Gonzalez held that "a credible threat that causes a person to abandon lawful political or religious associations or beliefs is persecution".[26]

ii. The U.S. Seventh Circuit also states that the forbidding of particular religious observance is the essence of persecution. In Bucar v. INS, the Seventh Circuit held that "it is the definition of religious persecution that the votaries of a religion are forbidden to practice it."[27]

Nationality

This term is not the same as "citizenship". Nationality includes:

i. membership of a specific cultural, ethnic and/or linguistic group

ii. common geographical origins

iii. common political origins[28]

For example, Kurds living in Turkey, Iraq, Syria or Iran constitute a national group.

Membership of a particular social group

A social group may relate to a specific country or may be defined by international human rights law.[29] This category is often mutable in form to reflect evolving society.

The UNHCR defines a particular social group as:

a group of persons who share a common characteristic other than their risk of being persecuted, or who are perceived as a group by society. The characteristic will often be one which is innate, unchangeable, or which is otherwise fundamental to identity, conscience or the exercise of one's human rights.

This definition includes characteristics which are historical and therefore cannot be changed, and those which, though it is possible to change them, ought not to be required to be changed because they are so closely linked to the identity of the person or are an expression of fundamental human rights. It follows that sex can properly be within the ambit of the social group category with women being a clear example of a social subset defined by innate and immutable characteristics, and who are frequently treated differently to men.

If a claimant alleges a social group that is based on a characteristic determined to be neither unalterable or fundamental, further analysis should be undertaken to determine whether the group is nonetheless perceived as a cognizable group in that society. So, for example, if it were determined that owning a shop or participating in a certain occupation in a particular society is neither unchangeable nor a fundamental aspect of human identity, a shopkeeper or members of a particular profession might nonetheless constitute a particular social group if in the society they are recognized as a group which sets them apart[30]

In this category, women can qualify as members in a particular social group if they are persecuted because of their gender.[31] Another example of a particular social group would be Christians within a Muslim-majority context: for example Armenian Christians in Turkey, Coptic Christians in Egypt, and Syrian Orthodox Christians in Syria.

Defining what is meant by a "particular social group"

It could be argued that Christians in a Muslim-majority context could be defined as a particular social group, as Islam has a propensity to view itself as a political and social system as well as a religion. A discussion of Muslim political identity is beyond the scope of the present study, but it does give a window of understanding (and possibly a basis for argument) that may lead to religious minorities being understood as a distinct social group as well as a religious one. For this reason, it may be important to apply for refugee status on the basis of more than one Convention ground where the evidence permits.

The House of Lords, which is the highest appeal court for England and Wales, defined a particular social group as

one consisting of persons who share an immutable characteristic, that is to say a characteristic that is beyond the power of the individual to change or is so fundamental to individual identity or conscience that it ought not to be required to be changed. A characteristic which is beyond the power of the individual to change may be innate or may consist of a shared past experience.[32]

The Supreme Court of Canada gave a similar definition for "particular social group" in the seminal case Attorney-General of Canada v. Ward. The Court held that

[a] good working rule for the meaning of "particular social group" provides that this basis of persecution consists of three categories: (1) groups defined by an innate, unchangeable characteristic; (2) groups whose members voluntarily associate for reasons so fundamental to their human dignity that they should not be forced to forsake the association; and (3) groups associated by a former voluntary status, unalterable due to its historical permanence.[33]

Both these definitions note the fundamental dignity of conscience and indicate that a group should not be forced to deny their fundamental beliefs and/or abandon their history as a centuries-old faith community. This is relevant for Christian communities, particularly those living within the Muslim context.

First, the Christian community, in a context of persecution, can argue that its members have freely decided to be Christians and that religious belief is a fundamental freedom. Therefore they should not be asked to forsake it.

Second, in the case of denominations that have existed for centuries (Copts, Syrian Orthodox, Chaldean Catholic, etc.), it should also be argued that the Christian community has a "historical permanence" or "shared past experience" that should not be disturbed.

For converts to Christianity, it may be more relevant to use the first argument, while those Christians from ancient denominations should make use of both.

Political opinion

The holding of political opinion encompasses the exercise of a number of fundamental freedoms, including freedom of thought, opinion, expression and association. All of these are protected freedoms under international human rights law. This is the background for the protection of political opinion under the Refugee Convention.

Political opinion includes any opinion on any matter in which the machinery of state, government and policy may be engaged[34] or any action perceived to challenge governmental authority.[35] An individual must hold a political opinion that has come to the attention of the authorities or stands a reasonable possibility of becoming known to the state. For instance, the individual may be a member of a political party that wants to start democratic reforms, and this membership may make the individual a target of a repressive regime.

A political opinion may be expressed through political action or activity, or it may be implied or imputed to the applicant by the authorities.[36] For example, a student may attend a protest against actions of the government. As a result the government may believe that the student is a member of the opposition political party and threaten to arrest him.

A political opinion may also take the form of certain behaviour, depending on the circumstances in the country. For example, a woman might drive a car in contravention of a law created by a government that prohibits all women from driving cars in the country. Attempts to exercise a fundamental human right that is forbidden in the country, such as freely choosing to follow a religion of one's choice, also fall into this category.

"[T]he person must be outside the country of his or her nationality or, if stateless, outside the country of his or her formal habitual residence"

This element of the fivefold test is very straightforward. In order to be eligible for refugee status, an individual must have left the country from which relief is sought. This requirement is not met if the individual remains in their country of origin or, in the case of stateless persons, remains in their place of habitual residence.[37]

So, for example, if a citizen of Iraq has fled to Jordan and upon arrival in Jordan applies for refugee status, the condition is met.

Case law regarding nationality/statelessness

It is much easier to handle claims from individuals who have left a state with which the individual has some evidence of citizenship or long-term residence.

The issue becomes more complicated when the refugee applicant is stateless. In this case, establishing the "country of former habitual residence" becomes an important determination.

The Canadian Federal Court considered this issue in its decision in Maarouf v. Canada.[38] The Court stated,

> *The definition of "country of former habitual residence" should not be unduly restrictive so as to pre-empt the provision of "surrogate" shelter to a stateless person who has demonstrated a well-founded fear of persecution on any of the enumerated grounds. A country of former habitual residence should not be limited to the country where the claimant initially feared persecution. The argument that habitual residence necessitates the claimant be legally able to return to that state is contrary to the shelter rationale underlying international refugee protection.*
>
> *Once a stateless person has abandoned the country of his former habitual residence for the reasons indicated in the definition, he is usually unable to return. The concept of "former habitual residence" seeks to establish a relationship to a state which is broadly comparable to that between a citizen and his country of nationality. Thus the term implies a situation where a stateless person was admitted to a country with a view to a continuing residence of some duration, without necessitating a minimum period of residence. The claimant must have established a significant period of de facto residence in the country in question.*

"[T]he person must be unable or, owing to such fear, unwilling to avail him or herself of the protection of that country"

Either the claimant must be prevented by circumstances beyond his control (including a civil war, coup d'état or international armed conflict) from returning to his home country, or his fear of harm must make him unwilling to return (e.g. a convert from Islam to Christianity who fled from his country after receiving numerous death threats from neighbours and family members).

Furthermore, the state may have withheld protection from the claimant or is unable to protect the claimant from non-state actors who may inflict harm on him. For instance, in the case of Afghanistan, the national government does not control all areas within its borders. In some regions, the Taliban is the real government. Even if Afghanistan wanted to provide protection to individuals, it would be unable to do so, because the Taliban controls certain areas of the country.

Failure of state protection is a fundamental reason for the Refugee Convention. It is therefore an important fact to establish in order to obtain refugee status.

Case law related to sufficiency of protection

In Canada (Attorney General) v. Ward, the Supreme Court of Canada held:

> *[t]he test as to whether a state is unable to protect a national is bipartite: (1) the claimant must subjectively fear persecution; and (2) this fear must be well-founded in an objective sense.*
>
> *The claimant need not literally approach the state unless it is objectively unreasonable for him or her not to have sought the protection of the home authorities.*
>
> *The Immigration and Refugee Board, if the claimant's fear has been established, is entitled to presume that persecution will be likely and that the fear is well-founded if there is an absence of state protection.*
>
> *The presumption goes to the heart of the inquiry, which is whether there is a likelihood of persecution. The persecution must be real – the presumption cannot be built on fictional events – but the well-foundedness of the fears can be established through the use of such a presumption.*

The claimant must provide clear and convincing confirmation of a state's inability to protect absent an admission by the national's state of its inability to protect that national. Except in situations of complete breakdown of the state apparatus, it should be assumed that the state is capable of protecting a claimant. This presumption, while it increases the burden on the claimant, does not render illusory Canada's provision of a haven for refugees. It reinforces the underlying rationale of international protection as a surrogate, coming into play where no alternative remains to the claimant.[39]

In the UK, the House of Lords considered the issue of the sufficiency of protection in the case of Horvath v. Secretary of State for the Home Department also. The Lords stated that

In the context of an allegation of persecution by non-state agents, the word "persecution" implies a failure by the state to make protection available against the ill- treatment or violence which the person suffers at the hands of his persecutors. [...] The primary duty to provide the protection lies with the home state. It is its duty to establish and to operate a system of protection against the persecution of its own nationals. If that system is lacking the protection of the international community is available as a substitute. But the application of the surrogacy principle rests upon the assumption that, just as the substitute cannot achieve complete protection against isolated and random attacks, so also complete protection against such attacks is not to be expected of the home state. The standard to be applied is therefore not that which would eliminate all risk and would thus amount to a guarantee of protection in the home state. Rather it is a practical standard, which takes proper account of the duty which the state owes to all its own nationals."[40]

Exclusions

In order to be formally classified as a refugee, as defined in the previous section, the refugee applicant must provide factual information to satisfy each element of the refugee definition.

In this section, we will discuss the Convention exclusions that will act to disqualify an individual from classification as a refugee and that are contained in articles 1D – 1F of the 1951 Convention.

Articles 1D and 1E state that certain types of people, although they would typically qualify as refugees, are excluded from refugee status due to UNHCR's determination that they are not in need of international protection.

Article 1D excludes those individuals who are already receiving protection from another branch of the UN system. For instance, Palestinian refugees who are under the protection of the United Nations Works and Relief Agency (UNWRA) are not eligible for protection by UNHCR.

Article 1E excludes those individuals who have been recognised by the authorities of another country in which they have taken residence as having the same rights and obligations as nationals in that country. For Article 1E to apply, the individual must enjoy status akin to that of a national.

Article 1F operates to exclude individuals on the basis that they do not deserve protection from the UN system because there are serious grounds to believe that the individual has committed:

Article 1F(a): a war crime or a crime against humanity

Article 1F(b): a serious non-political crime outside the country of refuge and prior to admission to that country as a refugee

Article 1F(c): an act contrary to the purposes and principles of the United Nations

The UNHCR guidance is that Article 1F must be applied restrictively and after careful consideration.

Cessation

Under Article 1C of the Convention, formal determination as a refugee may be temporary in certain circumstances: if the individual refugee

i. Voluntarily accepts the protection of his/her country of nationality

ii. Voluntarily re-acquires his/her nationality after losing it

iii. Acquires a new nationality and enjoys the protection of that country

iv. Voluntarily re-establishes himself/herself in the country he/she fled because of fear of persecution

v. Can no longer refuse to accept the protection of this country because the circumstances that led to recognition as a refugee have ceased to exist

vi. Has no nationality but can no longer refuse to accept the protection of his/her country of habitual residence because the circumstances that led to recognition as a refugee have ceased to exist

The first four cessation scenarios involve a decision of the refugee to abandon international protection by submitting to a particular nationality.

The final two cessation scenarios involve a change of conditions within the refugee's home country.

Conclusion

In this section, you have been introduced to the four elements of the definition of refugee status according to the Convention and the Protocol. Moreover, these elements have been presented from the perspective of religious persecution and how court decisions from various resettlement countries define various parts of the refugee definition. This section also introduced the two key concepts of exclusion and cessation. Exclusion will prevent a refugee applicant from receiving refugee protection owing to the applicant's wrongful acts. Cessation will revoke refugee status if the refugee protection is no longer needed. Having completed this section, you will now understand the factual criteria that are applied in establishing whether an individual meets the test for Refugee Status Determination. In the next section we will look at how these criteria are applied during the interview process.

REFUGEE STATUS DETERMINATION

PROCEDURAL OVERVIEW

In this section, the reader will be introduced to each of the stages involved in the Refugee Status Determination (RSD) process and the practical ways in which either individuals, church groups or organisations can provide support to refugee applicants who are going through the RSD process.

The key stages in the Refugee Status Determination process are:

1. Reception at NGO
2. Registration with UNHCR
3. UNHCR Interview
4. Receipt of Refugee Status
5. Appeal Process
6. Request to Re-Open File

Diagram 1-2 provides an overview of the basic procedures involved in the RSD process. It includes three phases: registration (yellow), successful recognition or appeal (blue), rejection and file closing (red):

Yellow card/Asylum seeker certificate: this is evidence that the refugee applicant has registered with UNHCR and has applied for RSD and is awaiting the determination. This document shows local authorities, particularly the police, that the applicant is under the interim protection of UNHCR until the RSD process has been completed.

Blue card/Refugee recognition: this document accompanies the recognition of the individual as a refugee and is supposed to alert local authorities to the refugee's rights to remain in the country until an appropriate durable solution (return to country of origin, integration in host country, or third country resettlement) is found for the refugee. Possession of a blue card means that the refugee, according to UNHCR, is to be afforded all the rights and protections enjoyed by citizens in the host country. In sum, once in possession of a blue card the individual is to be treated like a citizen of the host country.

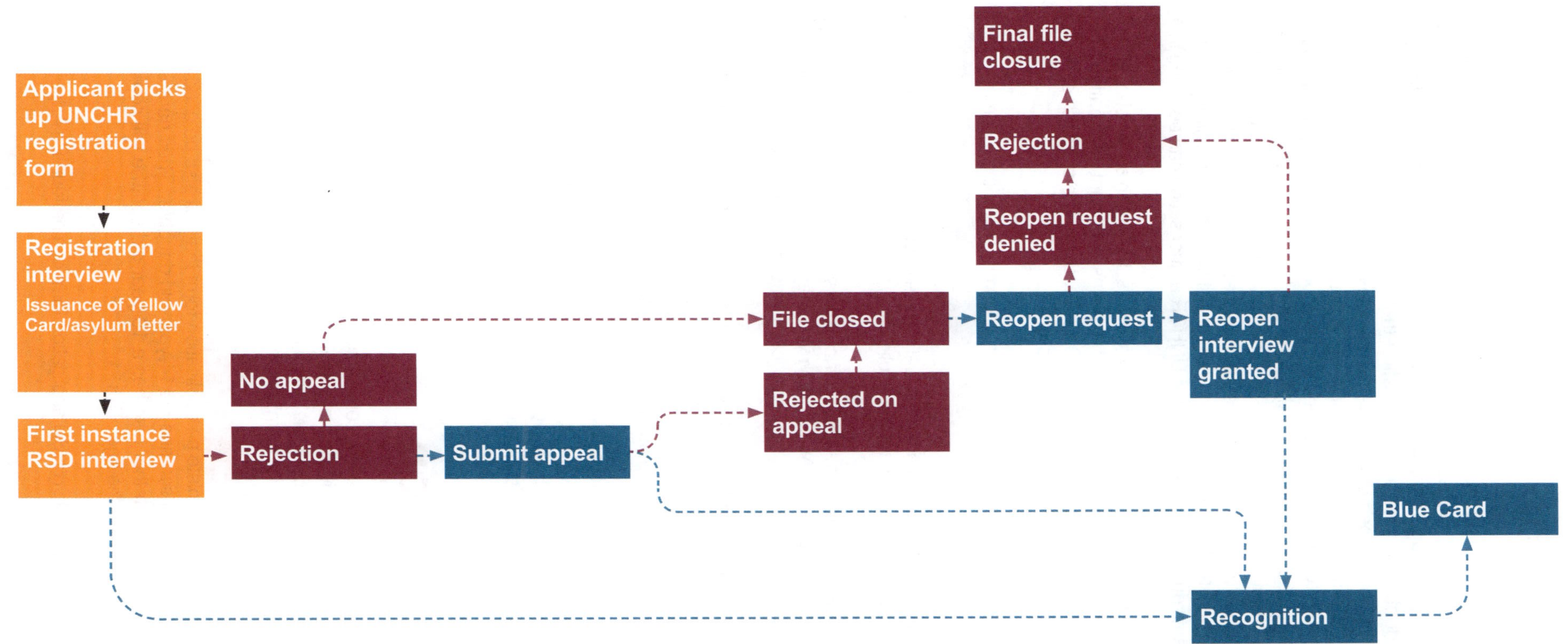
Applicant picks up UNCHR registration form
Registration interview
Issuance of Yellow Card/asylum letter
First instance RSD interview
Rejection
No appeal
Submit appeal
File closed
Rejected on appeal
Reopen request
Reopen request denied
Rejection
Final file closure
Reopen interview granted
Recognition
Blue Card

1. Reception at NGO

If you are an organisation that has been established with the intention of providing support for applicants going through the RSD process, you will need to start by collecting and processing information from the refugee applicant. Appendix A provides a sample intake form that you may wish to adopt. If you are an organisation that also assists with any legal matters, you should have two other types of document signed by the refugee applicant. These are the preliminary registration agreement (Appendix B) and various confidentiality waivers. The general confidentiality agreement (Appendix C) authorises the named organisation to release confidential information to UNHCR in relation to the applicant's refugee claim, and to act on the applicant's behalf with the UNHCR. The specific confidentiality agreement (Appendix D) allows the organisation to release confidential information to specifically named individuals or organisations. The UNHCR authorisation is essential if you as an organisation are to represent refugee applicants during appeals. A sample UNHCR authorisation can be found in Appendix E.

In addition to intake collection and agreements/waivers, the organisation should provide a local Information Sheet for Refugee Applicants that explains important information about the local UNHCR field office procedures governing RSD applications. The specifics of such a sheet will be covered in the Country Specific Inquiries section.

Appendix F is a sample checklist for reception procedures. This is the recommended checklist to use during the initial reception stage.

If you are providing assistance as an individual or as a church, you may wish to consider what practical support you could provide for the applicant.

Many asylum seekers are forced to leave their country with the minimal of belongings and arrive in another country in great need. As a church you may wish to collect clothes and household items that may be used to meet the very practical needs of those seeking asylum.

Another area of need is access to services. You may consider establishing a database of volunteers in the community with relevant skills, such as lawyers, doctors, language teachers and interpreters, whom you can approach to play a role in providing care and assistance to those in need and to equip people with the most essential skills needed to start the process of integration.

Another key area of need for newcomers is church fellowship. As a church you may wish to hold lunches or dinners for asylum seekers as a means of encouraging their integration into the church family. You may also be able to hold Bible studies in their language if existing members of the congregation have the relevant language skills.

2. Registration

After the refugee applicant has been received, they should be directed to the nearest RSD office, where they should register. This is the first step in the RSD application. The applicant (and every family member who is 18 years or older) will be required to complete their own Refugee Status Determination Application. Family members under the age of 18 will be included in the RSD application made by the applicant.

For example, a father will complete an application form that will also be used to determine the applications of his 16-year-old son and his 14-year-old daughter. Their names will be included in his application form. If the father also has a 19-year-old son, he will complete a separate application form, as he is over the age of 18.

A sample of the standard UNHCR RSD application form can be found in Appendix G.

The application form requires the applicant to provide information on the following matters:

i. Education history

ii. Work history

iii. Any identification documents

iv. Any history of applying for refugee status

v. Travel route to host country

vi. Language preference for the interview

vii. Gender preference for interviewer and translator

viii. Reasons why applicant left home country

ix. Reasons why applicant is afraid to return to home country

In-country UNHCR offices often have their own policy on the procedure for the completion of the application form. Some offices require that the refugee applicant complete the application at the offices during specific registration sessions. Other UNHCR field offices engaged in the refugee determination process permit refugee applicants for refugee status determination to obtain the application form from the office and complete the form off-site. It is essential that you find out what regulations apply at the UNHCR office in your country. If the refugee applicant is required to complete the application form at the UNHCR office during a registration session, you will need to explain the application process to the individual prior to their attendance at the office in order for them to complete the application form.

The applicant should view the application form as an opportunity for them to persuade the decision-makers regarding the grounds for their application. Due care and attention should be given to the information that ought to be included in the form. Those completing the form should also understand what criteria the decision-makers will use to determine the application. That is why it is essential for there to be prior consideration of the Refugee Convention criteria that were discussed in section 1 of this handbook.

During the registration process:

i. The UNHCR will photograph all applicants.

ii. The applicant will be issued with an UNHCR Asylum Seeker Certificate (the Yellow Card) (see Appendix H). This certificate is proof that the refugee applicant has registered with UNHCR and is awaiting the outcome of their application for RSD. The yellow card is important, as it shows local authorities that the applicant is under the interim protection of the UNHCR until the RSD process has been completed.

iii. The time and date of the RSD interview will be identified and provided to the applicant.

A guide to completing the application form can be found in Appendix I.

3. UNHCR Refugee Status Determination interview[41]

The interview is probably the most important aspect of the determination process. An individual application for RSD will largely be decided upon the facts that the applicant puts forward during their interview. The interview also provides the decision-makers with an opportunity to assess the credibility of the applicant's claim for RSD.

A core objective for any support group, be it a church or a volunteer group of advocates, at this stage is to assist the refugee applicant to prepare for the UNHCR interview. It is very important to remember that the applicant is likely to feel very vulnerable given the enormous uncertainties they face and perhaps also the circumstances in which they have fled their home country.

In anticipation of the RSD interview, the NGO / organisation / supporters may consider holding mock interviews with the refugee applicant as a means of enabling them to present their application for refugee status determination as well as possible. A mock interview may provide the refugee applicant with an opportunity to consider how best to answer the type of questions he will be asked during the RSD interview. It will also provide supporters / the NGO with an opportunity better to understand the strengths and weaknesses of the refugee applicant's application. Thus it provides an opportunity to consider if further evidence in support of the application can be obtained in advance of the interview.

By whatever means, it is essential that you work to assist the applicant to identify all the factual information that can be relied upon to meet the criteria for refugee status determination and allow them an opportunity to consider how best to present that information. Encourage the applicant also to consider body language and the role that plays in establishing rapport with the decision-makers. This includes the importance of maintaining eye contact and ensuring arms are not folded, which may convey a defensive attitude.

A sample questionnaire that could be used for a mock RSD interview can be found in Appendix J.

Pre-interview preparation

In advance of the interview date, the refugee applicant should make copies of all documents relating to the refugee claim and bring **originals** of all documentation to the interview.

If legal representation has been secured, the refugee applicant should coordinate with the legal representative to ensure they are present at the interview.

If a legal representative has not been secured, someone else can attend alongside the applicant as a source of advice, support and encouragement during the process. If you are a church, you could create a list of suitable people who are willing to accompany applicants to the interview. All volunteers should be trained so that they understand the process and issues involved before they are permitted to accompany refugee applicants to the interview.

In advance of the interview, ensure that the applicant understands the purpose of the interview: to identify whether the facts of their particular case fall within the specified grounds that exist under the Convention for refugee status.

Explain that the interviewer will at times ask probing questions and will be looking for detailed information. The more detailed the answers that can be given, the more persuasive is the applicant's account likely to be in the eyes of the interviewer.

The refugee applicant should arrive early on the morning of the scheduled interview. The refugee applicant should be advised that it may take several hours before the interview commences and it would be prudent to make sure that they have with them a supply of food and water.

On average, the interview should last between two and four hours. In exceptional circumstances, the interview could last all day.

During the interview[42]

Note the following vital points:

i. If an interpreter is present, make sure at the start of the interview that the applicant understands the interpreter. If not, the applicant should indicate that they cannot understand the interpreter.

ii. If the applicant thinks that the interpreter is not correctly translating their answers they should make this known as soon as it becomes apparent during the course of the interview, not afterwards.

iii. The applicant must put before the interviewer all the information that will assist in meeting the criteria (as discussed above) for refugee status.

iv. The applicant must avoid any temptation to make up facts.

v. The facts relied upon in the interview should correspond to the information contained in the RSD application form.

vi. The applicant must give as much detail as is possible during the interview concerning the events that forced the applicant to leave their home country and that make the applicant fearful of persecution should they be returned.

vii. The applicant should recount events in chronological order. If there is uncertainty about the actual dates, approximate dates should be used.

viii. The applicant should say where the events happened.

ix. The applicant should identify any perpetrators of harmful acts against the applicant. If the applicant does not know an offender's name, a description of the offender's appearance should be given, along with any information that may establish if the perpetrators are fellow citizens or were acting in an official / governmental capacity.

x. The applicant should say how often the events occurred.

xi. The applicant should provide information about any steps taken to seek protection from the state and the results of those steps. For example: attempts to report incidents to the police, human rights commission or local political representative.

xii. The applicant should recount the consequences / results of filing official complaints.

xiii. Copies of any forms completed should be submitted if the applicant has them.

xiv. Be polite and show respect to the UNHCR staff at all times:

- Remind the applicant immediately beforehand that the interviewer is likely to ask difficult questions. These questions are aimed at establishing the truthfulness of the applicant's explanation

- The applicant must **avoid** becoming defensive as a result of the questions.
- The interviewer is likely to be case-hardened, which means that they may appear unsympathetic to the facts of the applicant's case. This should not be taken personally by the applicant.
- A danger with interviewers who are case-hardened is that they may assume facts that do not apply in this particular case. Any legal advisor present during the interview should be alert to this.

xv. Never attempt to bribe UNHCR staff.

xvi. The Applicant should make sure they understand each question before providing their answer.

xvii. If the applicant suspects that either the interpreter or the interviewer is biased, they have a **right** to have them replaced by a different interpreter and/or interviewer. The interview will be postponed until new staff can be scheduled.

xviii. The applicant should give clear answers and be as precise as possible about the factual circumstances.

xix. The applicant should tell the interviewer all important facts about their case, even if they were not directly asked about these facts in the interview.

xx. The applicant should tell the interviewer if they used false documents and explain why such documents were used.

xxi. The applicant should inform the interviewer if at any time the applicant needs to take a comfort break during the interview process.

xxii. The applicant should inform the interviewer of any injuries or marks on their body related to the case. If possible, copies of medical examinations and/or photographs of marks or injuries should be available for the interviewer to review.

xxiii. At the end of the interview, the applicant should bring up any points they believe are relevant to their application but which have not already been covered during the interview.

xxiv. At the end of the interview, the applicant should be given an opportunity to have the interview transcript read aloud to the applicant so that any mistakes or missing information in the transcript can be corrected.

xxv. The applicant should ask for an indication as to when a decision may be made.

xxvi. The applicant should provide the interviewer with a reliable postal address which can be used for the decision letter.

Post-interview

Immediately after the interview, the applicant should make a note of the entire interview process. Most notably, the applicant (and/or legal representative) should record:

i. The names of the interviewer and interpreter

ii. The start and end times of the interview

iii. Concerns / problems with the interpreter and how these were addressed during the interview

iv. Concerns / problems with the interviewer and how these were addressed during the interview

v. The facts that were relied upon during the interview

vi. Subject matters that were the focus of questioning by the interviewer

vii. Any fear or apprehension experienced by the applicant due to the interviewing conditions

viii. Any subject areas of the applicant's testimony that may have been overlooked

ix. Whether the applicant felt they had a reasonable opportunity to present their case

Any concerns that might exist about the process adopted during the interview should be raised immediately with the UNHCR staff. If the concerns are very serious (for example an allegation of bias or intimidation by the interpreter / interviewer), these should be raised with the most senior staff within the UNHCR with a request for an interview to be scheduled with a different interviewer and interpreter and that the allegation be fully investigated.

After the interview, the applicant should be reminded that it may take months or even years for a RSD decision to be issued.

The applicant should meet with the organisation / you to de-brief after the interview. A file should be created with a record of the RSD interview included.

The status of the application can be checked by calling the UNHCR office directly. In order to do this you will need to reference the applicant's case number. In some locations, applicants may be able to check the status of their application via the internet.

Lodging complaints about the RSD process

Each office should have well-defined procedures for addressing RSD irregularities. The detail of these procedures should be available in publicly accessible documents.

As a general rule, if any problems do arise during the interview, complaints should be directed to the local UNHCR protection officer. Any complaints should be lodged as soon after the interview as is feasible. The longer the time period that is left before a complaint is lodged, the less serious / less persuasive it is likely to be considered by the UNHCR Office.

If serious problems are widespread, a complaint should be lodged with the inspector general of the UNHCR in Geneva, Switzerland.

4. Receipt of refugee status

If the applicant is determined to be a refugee, the UNHCR will grant the refugee a UNHCR Refugee Certificate. A sample UNHCR Refugee Certificate is found in Appendix K.

The refugee will be referred to the Durable Solutions Department to determine what course of action is appropriate for the refugee.

A durable solution provides the refugee with an opportunity to rebuild their life. There are three durable solutions, according to UNHCR practices:

i. repatriation (return to the home country when it is determined that it is safe for the refugee to go back),

ii. local integration (refugee rebuilds his/her life within the host country)

iii. resettlement (refugee relocated to a country that receives refugees)

Most refugees will be either repatriated or integrated locally. Only 1% of refugees are resettled.

If a refugee is selected for resettlement, they will be directed by the UNHCR to a resettlement country. The main resettlement countries are Canada, the United States and Australia. The refugee should be prepared for another application process with the embassy of the country of resettlement.

The refugee should now have all the same rights and responsibilities as the citizens of the host country. The type of assistance available – housing, food, health care, work and education – varies from country to country and may vary from region to region within a country. Effort should be made to contact other organisations to see what they know of the available services for refugees.

The refugee should be made aware of the long wait associated with resettlement. Refugees could be waiting for years to be relocated to a resettlement country. Organisations should be aware of the general procedures followed by the resettlement countries.

The Inter-governmental Consultation on Migration, Asylum and Refugees (IGC) has published a very helpful resource on resettlement country practices regarding refugees/asylum seekers. It is titled *Asylum Procedures – Report on Policies and Practices in IGC Participating States* and can be requested free of charge by emailing IGC at info@igc-publications.ch.

5. Appealing a negative RSD decision[43]

If the UNHCR determines that the refugee applicant does not qualify for refugee status, they will send the refugee applicant a Notification of Negative RSD Decision. Appendix L contains a sample Notification of Negative RSD Decision.

The negative RSD decision generally has pre-printed grounds for denial of refugee status. The UNHCR will simply check the reason(s) for rejection and usually will not provide more specific reasons for rejection.

If you are an established organisation, you may be able to call the UNHCR office and inquire into the more specific reasons for denial of the application.

From the date of receipt of the letter, the applicant has 30 days to file an appeal against the decision.

It is therefore very important that the applicant/appellant makes a note of the date of when the letter was received and keeps the envelope as that often indicates the date the letter was processed by the postal services.

An appeal application form (see Appendix M) should be included with the Notification of Negative RSD Decision. If it is not included, please make contact with the UNHCR Office immediately to request a copy.

The appeal process involves the drafting of an appeal letter and attending an appeal interview.

The appeal letter[44]

The appeal letter should be written on the Appeal Application Form or should be attached to the Appeal Application Form. The refugee applicant should include photocopies of any documents related to the claim that were received after the UNHCR interview and have not yet been submitted to UNHCR.

As a general rule, the appeal letter **should not be longer than one page**. If there have been significant changes in the refugee's circumstances related to the claim with additional evidence of refugee status, it is acceptable to write a longer appeal letter.

Before drafting the appeal letter consideration must be given to how the applicant can overcome the grounds relied upon by the UNHCR in the refusal decision. The purpose of the appeal letter should be to demonstrate to the decision-maker why the application for RSD should be allowed on appeal.

The appeal letter should be drafted as follows:

- **i.** Introduction – "To the UNHCR, Branch Office __________. The UNHCR has denied my application to be recognized as a refugee, and this letter is an appeal of that decision."
- **ii.** Personal details – Insert the full name and UNHCR file number of the refugee applicant.
- **iii.** Details about the refugee claim – Four or five sentences summarizing the reasons why the applicant left their home country and why they are afraid to return. If there was information that the applicant was unable to provide during the interview, it should be included with an explanation of why it could not be provided at the interview.
- **iv.** Interview Conditions – If the refugee applicant felt uncomfortable or intimidated during the interview, the reasons for this should be included. Any steps taken to raise these concerns at the time of the interview should also be included.
- **v.** New Information – If the refugee applicant has any new information that was discovered after the initial UNHCR interview, they should include it, explain how they found the information and why it supports their refugee claim.
- **vi.** Developments in Home Country – The circumstances existing in the home country may have changed since the initial UNHCR interview took place. If these changed circumstances confirm or make worse the risk of persecution if the applicant is returned, they should be included in the letter.
- **vii.** If the refugee applicant has protection problems (security concerns or serious health problems) in the host country, the applicant should explain these problems in two or three sentences.
- **viii.** Conclusion – "For the reasons stated in this letter, I think that UNHCR should reconsider my case and I request that UNHCR grant me an appeal interview and protection." The refugee applicant should add their signature and the date of the appeal letter.

Further guidance on the drafting of the appeal letter is available in Appendix N.

The appeal interview[45]

The appeal interview will take a similar format to the initial UNHCR interview. The questions of the interviewer will be restricted to the matters raised on appeal, which means the interview is likely to be shorter than the initial UNHCR interview.

For this reason, it is important that in preparation for the appeal interview the applicant and those supporting him ensure they understand why the application was refused in the first instance and that the applicant is able to provide positive information to overcome the reasons for refusal.

Legal representation should be permitted for the appeal interview.

The applicant should be made aware that it may take months or even years for the UNHCR to issue a written decision on the appeal. The outcome will be communicated to the applicant in a letter.

If the appeal is successful, the applicant will be granted refugee status and will be issued with a Blue Card. The next stage will be consideration of durable solutions.

If the appeal is denied, the refugee applicant's file will be closed. The next stage will be removal to the home country. Removal will be effected by the state authorities rather than UNHCR staff.

The organisation should contact legal counsel and/or other organisations in the host country to determine what steps if any may be taken in response to a final denial of a refugee application. In Turkey,[46] for instance, there exists a possibility of temporary asylum, which may be granted by the local police commission. Furthermore, the Turkish government allows access for such applicants to an administrative court.[47] This inquiry should be covered by the general subject inquiry 3 in the Country Specific Inquiries section B below.

6. Re-opening a closed file

Once an applicant's file has been closed after an unsuccessful appeal there is very little that can be done. In exceptional circumstances, it may be possible to have an applicant's case re-opened.

The specific circumstances that may warrant the re-opening of a file include:

- **i.** New and reliable information showing a material change in either the personal circumstances of the applicant and/or conditions in the applicant's home country
- **ii.** Concrete evidence that the applicant's case was not properly decided in law
- **iii.** The UNHCR has a serious reason to believe that the administration of the applicant's case was not properly handled or the case was not fully examined

A real-life example of a successful application to reopen a failed application for RSD concerns an individual who fled her home country due to levels of violence she experienced as a woman. The woman made an application for RSD via the UNHCR. Her application failed in the first instance and on appeal, which meant that her case was formally closed by the UNHCR. She remained in the country, however, albeit living in fear of arrest and deportation at any point. During her time in the country she was provided with an opportunity to learn about the Christian faith, as a result of which she chose to convert to Christianity. After her conversion she wrote to the UNHCR seeking a reconsideration of her request for RSD status based on a material change in her circumstances, namely that she had converted to the Christian faith, something that would put her life in serious danger were she to be returned to her country of nationality.

As a result of the information she provided in her letter the UNHCR reopened her case and she was granted RSD.

Any request to re-open a file should be made in writing to the UNHCR Office.

The following is a suggested format for a request to reopen a closed case:

i. Introduction – "To the UNHCR, Branch Office __________. The UNHCR has denied my appeal to be recognized as a refugee, and this letter is a request to re-open my file."

ii. Personal details – Full name and UNHCR file number of refugee applicant.

iii. New Information –

- Account of the new information regarding changes in the applicant's personal circumstances and/or conditions in their home country

- Why this information amounts to a material change in circumstances that warrants the reopening of an application for RSD. For example: The applicant fled their home country to a third country where they made an application for RSD, which was refused in the first instance and on appeal. The applicant remained in the third country and as a result of community support had an opportunity to learn about the Christian faith and chose to change their religion to Christianity. Their home country is one that prosecutes those who change their religion. Therefore there is a real risk of persecution based on religion if they are returned to their home country. This is a material change of circumstances that might be considered as warranting the reopening of an application for RSD.

- Evidence, from either the applicant or the UNHCR, that the applicant's case was improperly handled or the case was not fully examined

iv. Conclusion – "For the reasons stated in this letter, the UNHCR should re-open my file and I request that UNHCR grant me an interview for re-opening this file." The refugee applicant should add their signature and the date of the re-opening request.

A more expansive resource for drafting a request to re-open a file is available in Appendix O.

It may also be prudent to approach a local MP or other politicians to petition the UNHCR to reopen a particular case. Support for the case from local news sources, lawyers or other NGOs may also assist.

The more detail you are able to provide in the letter as to the nature of the material change in circumstances and how that fits with one of the grounds for classifying an individual as a refugee, the more likely you are to succeed in persuading the UNHCR to reopen the case.

COUNTRY-SPECIFIC INQUIRIES

You / your church / your organisation should make extensive inquiries regarding refugee issues in your particular country. Such an inquiry is likely to take some time but will result in the creation of an invaluable guide and reference source concerning key issues of relevance to the care and support of refugees. Such a guide should enable you and others to identify what steps need to be taken to address problems and make productive recommendations to the decision-makers at either UNHCR or national level.

Key sources of information are likely to include local lawyers and law-based NGOs who provide specialist advice on refugee and immigration law, churches with a ministry in asylum care, national government departments, political representatives and international organisations.

General subjects to include in an inquiry:

i. Who is responsible for the registration of asylum seekers/refugees? (e.g. UNHCR, a government ministry, an NGO, etc.)

ii. Who is responsible for initial decisions regarding refugee cases?

iii. Is there an appeals process in place? If so, who is responsible for deciding appeals? How many levels of appeals exist? May negative decisions be challenged in court? Does an appeal automatically stay (stop) a deportation order? What are the ways in which a deportation order can be challenged?

iv. What bodies of law govern the RSD process? (Create a list of legal sources that will provide a useful reference tool.)

Logistical questions:

v. What are the hours of registration for refugees, and where does registration take place?

vi. Are there certain days on which certain language groups are required to register?

vii. Are asylum seekers/refugees entitled to legal representation at any or all stages of the process? What are the criteria for an individual to act as legal representative?

viii. What official guides are available in the public domain that cover the local RSD process?

ix. What is the average timeline for a refugee case? From registration to interview? From interview to decision? What is the time limit for lodging an appeal (given that the UNHCR standards are 30 days from receipt of denial of refugee status)? What is the average time period for an appeal decision?

x. Are asylum seekers/refugees permitted to work while their cases are being adjudicated?

xi. Can children receive an education while their cases are being adjudicated?

Once you have found the answers to questions 1-11, these should be converted into a useful facts handout that can be made available to refugee applicants. The handout should also include a list of all the NGOs and other sources of assistance that are available for refugee applicants.[48] For instance, it should include help for non-RSD legal needs (low-cost legal assistance for civil or criminal matters), psychological and other health services, educational services, employment training and job services, and services tailored to the needs of women, children, the elderly and the disabled.

Make a hierarchical diagram of the authorities responsible for implementing the RSD process and their contact details. An example is noted below.

If UNHCR is responsible for RSD, create a similar diagram with the High Commissioner at the top and the individual protection officers at the bottom. You may also wish to do the same with any official church institutions that are involved in the care of refugees.

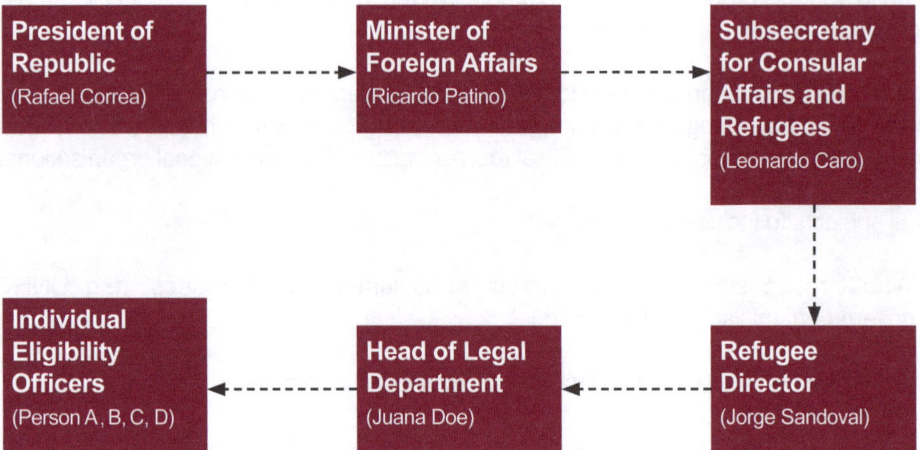

After research and creation of a hierarchal diagram, identify which people in the diagram you have access to.

xii. Compile a similar database to identify which (if any) other NGOs, universities, private lawyers or other organisations handle refugee cases. How can relations and links be created with these key institutions?

xiii. Who, within the refugee community, would you identify as a leader, or as a trustworthy source of information? What role can they undertake in providing assistance from within the refugee community?

xiv. Describe the relationship between UNHCR, the local government, the different NGOs, the refugee community and any other important actors.

Create a recording mechanism whereby you can monitor the outcome of the RSD applications. Key questions to answer are:

i. What are the grounds of refusal in the first instance for religious persecution applicants?

ii. What are the grounds for refusal on appeal? How many cases are successfully reopened?

iii. Are applications from particular countries favoured over others?

iv. What types of concerns are raised by applicants and their legal representatives during the interview process? Do any patterns form? How can these concerns best be resolved? From the hierarchical flow charts you have created, who would be the most appropriate people to raise these concerns with? How might you be able to work together to improve the treatment and assessment of refugee applications?

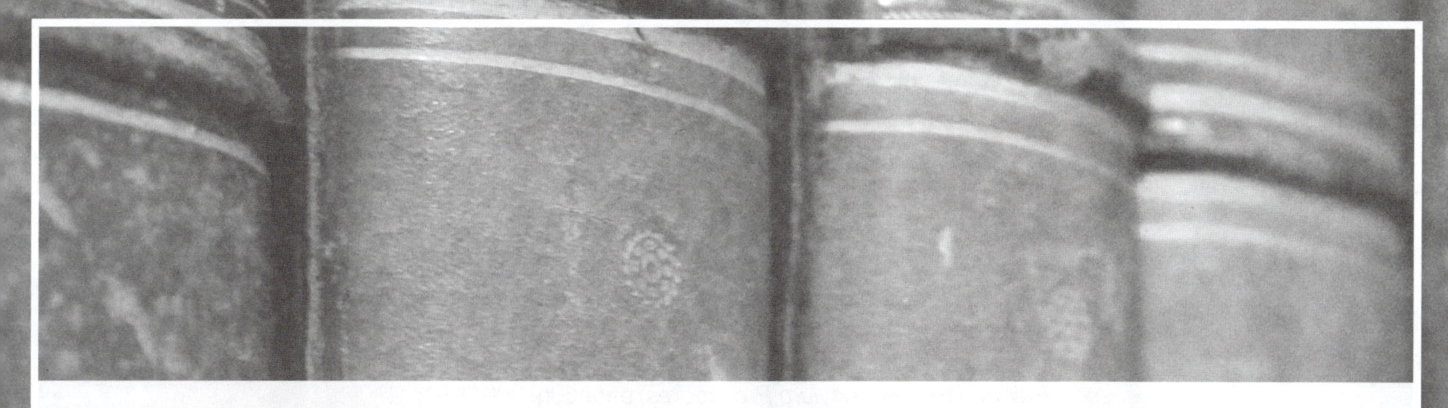

BEST PRACTICE FOR LEGAL ADVOCATES

Evaluation of advocates' knowledge base

As practice varies from country to country, UNHCR office to office, it is imperative that all legal advocates familiarise themselves with and satisfy the local requirements that govern representation for refugee applicants. The UNHCR has stressed that asylum seekers have a right to legal counsel "at all stages of the procedure" (UNHCR, *Asylum-Processes: Fair and Efficient Asylum Procedures*, para 50g, 2001).

In its own RSD procedures, UNHCR's standards allow asylum seekers to obtain the assistance of legal representatives and advisors (section 4.3.3). Generally speaking, refugee applicants are permitted to have a legal representative accompany them to their RSD interviews provided that they submit a standard consent form in advance of the interview. The legal representative may make brief remarks at the close of the interview. The representative should in general not interrupt the interview except in the case of "breaches of procedural fairness that could not be adequately addressed or remedied if they were raised in closing submissions" (section 4.3.3).

UNHCR guidelines also permit individual field offices to develop their own representative accreditation process for legal advocates. While UNHCR does not require the legal advocates to be accredited lawyers, it does require the advocates at least to have a "working knowledge" of refugee law and RSD procedures, experience assisting asylum seekers and knowledge of the applicant's claim (section 4.3.3).

UNHCR eligibility officers may refuse a legal representative if there is "good reason to believe that the third party is not qualified, or otherwise suitable" (section 4.3.3).

Familiarisation with the contents of this manual should provide a solid foundation for helping refugees. The overarching principles of refugee law have been addressed in the previous sections.

It is recommended that the advocate review additional resources related to refugee law. These include:

i. Handbook on Procedures and Criteria for Determining Refugee Status under the 1951 Convention and the 1967 Protocol relating to the Status of Refugees, http://www.unhcr.org/refworld/pdfid/3ae6b3314.pdf

ii. Self-Study Module 2: Refugee Status Determination. Identifying Who is a Refugee, http://www.unhcr.org/refworld/docid/43141f5d4.html

iii. Training videos from Asylum Access. Asylum Access has produced excellent overviews of refugee law and related issues. To access videos, email Asylum Access for more information at help@asylumaccess.org.

Refugee advocacy in RSD

First instance declaration

A month prior to the RSD interview, the refugee applicant should submit a first instance declaration.

In this document, the refugee applicant, with the help of the advocate, should include:

i. introductory information (name, UNHCR file no., nationality, ethnicity, religion, passport number, date and place of birth, marital status, languages, date of arrival, date of UNHCR registration, date of initial RSD interview and current telephone number)

ii. family history and background

iii. a testimony set out in the order of events

iv. the route taken to reach the host country

v. the factual basis for the fear of return

vi. a list of any documentary evidence

The declaration must be signed and dated with a declaration of the truth and accuracy of the content of the witness statement. A sample first instance declaration can be found in Appendix P.

This document is important, as it will be used by the interviewing officer in their preparation of the interview. Lawyers involved in the drafting of this document should consider what information is required for it to be as persuasive as possible when read by the interviewing officer. This document should start to persuade the interviewing officer to view this case favourably.

Therefore:

i. ensure that as much detail as possible is included

ii. be as specific as possible about the events and the fear

iii. use headings to make the declaration more persuasive

Opening/closing statements[49]

When accompanying the refugee applicant to the RSD interview, the legal advisor should be given the opportunity to make an opening statement before the interview begins and then make a closing statement at the conclusion of the interview. It must be noted that the 2005 procedural standards for RSD do not state a right to an opening or closing statement.

Although there is no stated right, the opening statement is very important to support the refugee applicant's case. It is the appropriate time for the legal advocate to note any health issues that may make the interview more complicated. The opening statement should be viewed as an opportunity by the lawyer to set the scene for what the applicant is going to say during the interview.

The entire opening statement should be recorded in the transcript by the eligibility officer, and the legal advocate should be reminded to remind the officer of the need for its inclusion in the transcript.

The following should be covered by the legal advocate in the opening statement:

i. Ask if the eligibility officer has read all submitted documents and whether they have any questions. In some occasions the eligibility officer may have read only parts of the testimony and legal submission, which may lead to confusion. Whether or not the eligibility officer refers to the submission, the material they have read will influence the interview. If they have not read any of the submission, the interview will be significantly different.[50]

ii. Briefly state the grounds that identify the applicant as a refugee. Without going into the details of the claim, state why the applicant is a refugee. This will also give the eligibility officer the context for the claim and therefore the information they ought to look for during the interview.

iii. Ask for a change of interpreter or eligibility officer if there is a problem with language, gender or the comfort of the applicant.

iv. Inform or remind the eligibility officer of any vulnerabilities or special criteria. By your identifying the applicant's special needs and criteria before the interview, the eligibility officer will know to be more sensitive to the applicant during the interview

v. Express any problems the applicant is likely to have during the interview. For example, the applicant may suffer from fatigue, memory loss, lack of comprehension of interview process and questions, hearing difficulties, paranoia or inability to answer questions clearly for reasons of trauma or other vulnerability. A person who is a victim of torture or a minor, or who has a fear of authorities, may also have difficulties communicating coherently during the interview.

vi. Report on any security or legal issues the applicant has experienced in the country of asylum. Reiterate security issues or other problems; make a request to expedite the claim and find a secure situation for the applicant; and raise any legal problems the applicant may have pertaining to his legal status in the country.

vii. Mention if the applicant has been detained, abused or threatened by authorities or other parties.

viii. In the case of an appeal or reopening interview, highlight any new information that the applicant is now in possession of. The opening statement is not the place to discuss all the new information that is submitted in an appeal, but it is important to draw the attention of the eligibility officer to any new information.

ix. Request special attention or services the applicant may need: for example, medical treatment, documentation of torture, psychological evaluation or material assistance.

x. Raise any other issues that need special attention.

xi. Thank the eligibility officer for allowing the applicant to be represented in the interview. Remember to be civil and friendly to the eligibility officer and all UNHCR staff. Show your appreciation for their cooperation with legal advisors. Indicate that the purpose of legal aid work, besides assisting the asylum seeker, is to help the UNHCR through the RSD process.

The legal representative should take a note of the entire content of the interview. They should make a note of any moments when information may have been misunderstood, or interpreted and/or recorded incorrectly. These moments should be clarified during the interview if there is an opportunity or at least at the close of the interview.

At the end of the interview, the legal advisor will have another opportunity to speak on behalf of the applicant. Speak slowly to allow the eligibility officer to record everything that is said.

The following are elements that should be included in your closing statement:[51]

i. Identify all key points that were made in statements, explaining anything that may have been unclear. The eligibility officer may wish to question the applicant on the issue/s.

ii. Add any important information that was not mentioned in the interview and is central to the claim. The eligibility officer may not have questioned the applicant on all the elements central to the claim. Highlight these points and allow the eligibility officer to question the applicant further. Make a note for future reference if the eligibility officer does not further question the applicant.

iii. Emphasise the important pieces of evidence and reiterate why these show there is a real fear of persecution if returned to their country of origin.

iv. Follow up on the requests made prior to the interview and during the opening statement. The eligibility officer may have researched possibilities for further material assistance or complimentary protection during the breaks. Ask if the eligibility officer knows what assistance the applicant can expect.

v. Ask if the eligibility officer has any questions for you as legal advisor.

vi. Ask when the applicant will receive a response on their claim. The applicant is entitled to receive the decision within one month in normal circumstances and up to three months in certain circumstances. Once a limited period has been defined by the eligibility officer, the UNHCR should work within that period.

vii. Check that the file contains the correct contact information for the applicant and for the legal advisor.

viii. Thank the eligibility officer again for "allowing" legal representation in the interview. Stress any good points of the interview: for example, the eligibility officer's kind attitude towards the applicant or for facilitating access to services.

For reference, a sample closing statement is available in Appendix Q.

3. Transcripts and interview observation[52]

It is important that the legal advocate takes a precise note of the interview and the timings and procedures followed at the UNHCR offices. This is relevant should the need arise to file a complaint based on procedural irregularity or unfairness. If your applicant's application is rejected in the first instance, the transcript will be an essential piece of information when preparing the appeal letter and the appeal hearing opening statement.

Transcripts should also be used to inform periodical discussions with the UNCHR on the reform or improvement of procedures and questioning on religious freedom cases.

Adhere to the following steps in keeping the transcript:

Procedural issues[53]

i. Record the precise time and details of all procedures. Keep a record of the times of arrival, the beginning and end of registration, interviews, interruptions, breaks, and other incidents that occur before, during and after the interview.

ii. Take a note of all conversations held with UNHCR staff, especially those with the eligibility officer, those relating to the case, operating procedures and any other information.

iii. Record everything that is said and done during admission, registration and interview. Take a detailed note of the sequence of questions, the exact questions asked by the eligibility officer and the responses given by the applicant.

iv. Try to ensure a verbatim note of the questions and answers. If it is not possible to catch the exact words, summarise what was said and make a note that it is not an exact quote.

v. Record everything that is said to you, the legal advisor, before, during and after the interview. Make special note of comments regarding the applicant made in the middle of question sequences.

vi. Note the reaction when the applicant does not understand or asks for clarification.

The interpreter[54]

i. Record the interpreter's name and any problems that arise as a result of the interpreting. It is important to record the relationship between the applicant and the interpreter.

ii. If the applicant does not fully understand the interpreter or does not feel comfortable with the interpreter, or the interpreter shows an adverse opinion of the applicant, this should be recorded.

iii. If the applicant requests a change in interpreter but the request is not fulfilled, note any variation in the applicant's demeanour, change in information given, and other reactions that may be related to the interpreter.

iv. Describe the demeanour of the interpreter. Does the interpreter appear to be afraid of the eligibility officer? Are they able to correct misunderstandings or ask for questions to be repeated with ease?

v. If you know the applicant's language, make sure the interpreter is properly interpreting the words of the applicant.

The eligibility officer[55]

i. Write down the name of the eligibility officer.

ii. Record any key incidents or breaches in procedures, their time, and the reactions of both the eligibility officer and the applicant.

iii. Describe the eligibility officer's demeanour and attitude towards the applicant. Take a detailed note of any negative behaviour. For example, if the eligibility officer interrupts or insults the applicant, or shows outward frustration or anger by sighing loudly, throwing papers, yelling, or any other forms of outward emotion, record this behaviour in detail.

iv. Record how the applicant is affected by the eligibility officer's behaviour and attitude.

Non-verbal responses[56]

i. Make a record of the non-verbal content of the interview.

- How at ease was the applicant made by the interviewer?
- What steps did the interviewer take to ensure that the atmosphere was non-combative and conducive to illuminating what is sensitive and often difficult subject matter?

ii. Describe any interference or noise disturbances coming from outside the room that may adversely affect the applicant's ability to tell their story or cause a distraction to either the eligibility officer or the interpreter. Examples would include an interview clearly audible in the next room, colleagues talking in the corridor, road or building maintenance, traffic, radio or television.

iii. Describe the body language and posture of the eligibility officer. Note how body language may contribute to the atmosphere of confidence or intimidation. Is there positive eye contact throughout the interview?

iv. Describe any audible but non-verbal sounds that are made by the applicant.

v. Describe any audible but non-verbal sounds that are made by the interpreter or the eligibility officer. Do they denote impatience, disbelief or boredom? What is their impact on the applicant?

In addition to the creation of a transcript, it may be helpful for the legal advocate to have a checklist of procedural requirements under the UNHCR's Procedural Standards for Refugee Status Determination under UNHCR Mandate ("UNHCR Procedural Standards"). A sample checklist for UNHCR Procedural Standards is available in Appendix R. Coupled with the transcript, this should provide the foundation for any appeal and can provide the basis for any initiatives that seek to provide for more effective procedures in RSD interview.

4. Appeal and reopening files[57]

Many individuals with legitimate claims to refugee status are rejected in the first instance. This may be because refugees do not have any assistance in understanding how their case will be decided and thus may not understand how to respond to the interviewer's questions.

Some applicants may suffer from post-traumatic stress disorder or other mental and emotional health problems that can hinder their ability to tell their stories in a clear, effective and compelling manner.

Interviewers may stop short of asking the questions that would reveal an applicant's need for refugee status, or the applicant may lack trust in the interviewer or the interpreter and the process and therefore fail to disclose all relevant information. Other factors such as negligence, discrimination, and corruption on the part of RSD officials, or within the government or RSD system, may cause worthy applicants to be rejected. For all of these reasons, the right to appeal a negative decision is an essential right of refugee applicants that the refugee's legal advisor must fight to uphold.

The appeals process will vary according to the country in which you are working and the body that governs the RSD process. For more specific guidance on drafting documents in support of appeal or for reopening of closed files, see pages 28-31. In addition, a sample appellate template and appellate brief are available in Appendices R and S respectively.

ISSUES SPECIFIC TO APPLICATIONS BASED ON CONVERSION TO CHRISTIANITY

The credibility of conversion is a central issue in religion-based applications for refugee status. The UNHCR guidelines advise those who are deciding applications based on conversion to assess carefully the truthfulness or authenticity of the applicant's conversion.

The focus here is conversion to Christianity from another religion. Those who exercise one of the most fundamental human rights by changing their religion face unique challenges. Sadly, for many, when their choice to convert to Christianity becomes public they are forced to flee their home and seek refuge in another country, because of either societal or government persecution.

Many of the cases that Barnabas Fund and many other charities have been involved with indicate that the case officers working both within the UNHCR system and within state systems tend to approach applications that are based on conversion to Christianity with some cynicism.

In order to overcome the obstacles that Christian converts face, it is therefore very important that applicants and those supporting them are able to provide information that demonstrates the truthfulness and authenticity of an individual's conversion. The more factual information that can be put before the decision-maker, the more likely they are to accept that this is an authentic conversion.

Examples of the factual evidence that will assist in proving the authenticity of someone's conversion include:

- **i.** Attendance at church services, Bible study groups, activities of a congregation, mentoring and participation in prayer groups
- **ii.** Involvement in other features of church life: home group, men's/women's fellowships, participation on rotas such as for reading, tea/coffee or flowers, welcoming team, verger responsibilities etc.
- **iii.** Participation of children in church events such as Sunday school and kids' club
- **iv.** Knowledge of aspects of the Bible, liturgy etc.
- **v.** Baptism / Confirmation (often the decision-maker will suggest this is a baptism of convenience; the statement should show why this is not so)
- **vi.** Participation in communion services
- **vii.** Evidence of formal membership of a particular church
- **viii.** A written copy of the applicant's testimony and its having been shared during a church service or event

Where possible a statement should also be provided from a church leader or a senior member of a church who is involved in helping the applicant grow in their understanding of the Christian faith. Such a statement will help to confirm independently as much of the information relied upon as is possible and will add credibility to the applicant's own evidence.

Research has shown that decision-makers often seek to establish the credibility of conversion by examining the individual's knowledge of the teaching of the religion to which they have converted, by assessing their answers to fact-based knowledge questions about their new religion.

The following questions were collated by the Evangelical Alliance (EA), which is a Christian NGO based in London. It undertook an investigation into the processing of conversion-based asylum applications processed by the United Kingdom (UK) Border Agency (UKBA), which is the agency responsible for immigration in the UK, and published their findings in the report "Altogether for Asylum Justice".[58] All of these questions had been used by the UKBA during interviews for asylum applications made by converts to Christianity.

For example:

i. How do you prepare a turkey for Christmas?

ii. What were the names of the thieves either side of Jesus as he was crucified?

iii. What fruit was the forbidden fruit?

iv. What were the names of Jesus' disciples?

v. What will happen around the world during the second coming?

vi. What are the Ten Commandments?

vii. What is your favourite part of the Bible?

viii. What is the period running up to Christmas called?

The reader will note that it is difficult to see how many of these questions play a positive role in establishing the truthfulness and accuracy of someone's conversion to Christianity.

The UNHCR provides guidance on applications for refugee status that are based on religious conversion and how best to assess the credibility and truthfulness of such applications. The UNHCR recommends the use of more open questions to establish the truthfulness of an individual's conversion. This was a recommendation also put forward by the EA to the UKBA. Examples of subjective questions that should be used include:

i. How did you become a Christian?

ii. Why did you choose to change your religion to Christianity?

iii. What difference has Jesus made to your life?

iv. What differences has being a Christian made to your life?

v. What values does the Bible promote?

If during your observations either during interviews or as a result of assisting applicants in other ways it appears that the decision-maker adopts a knowledge test approach, you may wish to suggest that more subjective questions are also used to assess the credibility of conversion. In doing so you may reference the best practice guidelines devised by the UNHCR.

Any questions adopted during the interview should also take account of the individual circumstances of the applicant and the circumstances surrounding their conversion.

Levels of knowledge of a particular religion may vary considerably depending on the individual's social, economic or educational background and/or their age or sex and the country from which they have fled. This factor should be brought to the attention of the interviewer. For example, the more hostile the country where the conversion took place is to religions, the harder it will be to access resources about a particular faith, including the scriptures of that faith.

As indicated above, individuals may be persecuted on the basis of their religion even though they have little or no substantive knowledge of its tenets or practices. A lack of knowledge may be explained by further research into the particular practices of that religion in the area in question or by an understanding of the subjective and personal aspects of the claimant's case. For instance, the level of repression against a religious group in a society may severely restrict the ability of an individual to study or practice what are considered key aspects of their religion.

It is important not to assume that the decision-maker has any prior knowledge about Christianity. Decision-makers can make unreasonable assumptions about Christians depending on their background: for example that a true Christian would be able to recite the books of the Bible. Always be alert to this when you are preparing a statement and when giving evidence.

If the individual has been baptised / confirmed, you will need to explain in plain English:

i. what baptism represents for Christians

ii. the declarations made by a candidate prior to baptism before the congregation

iii. the training / preparation sessions that are attended by each candidate before baptism and what is covered in those training sessions

Good practice here would include securing a short witness statement from another member of the church leadership who witnessed the baptism of the asylum seeker and can testify to the statements made by the asylum seeker prior to baptism.

It will be necessary to explain the worship pattern and the ethos / traditions of the particular church. Doing so should avoid the danger of Home Office officials using their own preconceptions to misjudge the asylum seeker. For example, an asylum seeker in a church that does not use liturgy during the service may naturally have very limited knowledge of liturgy.

It is also important to avoid using phrases that are meaningful within a church setting but which may not be understood outside. An example might the statement that the asylum seeker has come to "know Jesus Christ" or is now "born again". Instead try to ensure that plain and simple language is used that will be understood by your audience, for example, that the individual has chosen to change his religion from X to Christianity and is now a member of church C where he attends (list of activities).

CONVERSION POST-DEPARTURE AND UNHCR RSD

Individuals may convert to another religion after their departure from their home country. How does this affect their ability then to apply for RSD?

A useful case is that of Bastanipour v INS (1992) 980 F 2nd 1129 USCA (7th Circuit). The case concerned an Iranian who was convicted of drug-smuggling offences in the US. He served a prison sentence in the US, during which he converted to Christianity. He successfully applied for asylum in the US based on his conversion and a well-founded fear of persecution if returned to Iran.

Conversion post-departure is not a bar to RSD, as the law recognises that certain acts may create a *sur place* claim to refugee status. (*Sur place* refugees are those who were not refugees when they left their countries of origin, but who become refugees at a later date, owing to intervening events.) In such situations, the UNHCR is of the opinion that particular concerns arise regarding credibility that require a rigorous and in-depth examination of the circumstances and genuineness of the conversion.

The following factors have been identified by the UNHCR as particularly important in assessing applications for RSD that are based on a post-departure conversion. These are factors therefore that are important for any applicant to include in the written application form for RSD and to talk about during the interview:

i. the nature of and connection between any religious convictions held in the country of origin and those now held

ii. any disaffection with the religion held in the country of origin, for instance, because of its position on gender issues or sexual orientation

iii. how the claimant came to know about the new religion in the country of asylum

iv. his or her experience of the new religion

v. the applicant's mental state

vi. the existence of corroborating evidence regarding involvement in and membership of the new religion

The specific circumstances in the country of asylum and the individual case may justify additional probing into particular claims.

The UNHCR will be looking to establish if the conversion is true or whether it is simply "self-serving".

The UNHCR encourages caution and suspicion of systematic and organised conversions carried out by local religious groups in the country of asylum and suspect that these are specifically for the purposes of accessing resettlement options.

The UNHCR manual make the point that "coaching" or "mentoring" of claimants is commonplace, which means that the testing of knowledge is of limited value.

The core issues determining the credibility of any conversion are its motivations and the effects it has had on the claimant's life.

The test remains whether the claimant would have a well-founded fear of persecution on a Convention ground if returned to the country s/he has left. This is what the written application and the RSD interview should be focused on for every applicant.

The application and the interview should assess whether the conversion may come to the notice of the authorities of the person's country of origin and how this is likely to be viewed by those authorities.

So-called "self-serving" activities do not create a well-founded fear of persecution on a Convention ground in the claimant's country of origin, if the opportunistic nature of such activities will be apparent to all, including the authorities there, and serious adverse consequences will not result if the person is returned.

However, those conducting the UNHCR interview must give appropriate consideration to the consequences of return to the country of origin and any potential harm that might justify refugee status or a complementary form of protection. In the event that the claim is found to be self-serving but the claimant nonetheless has a well-founded fear of persecution on return, international protection is required.

For this reason, context is very important. You must view the interview as an opportunity for you to teach the interviewer about how the authorities and or fellow-citizens in the country of origin could use even the mere exposure to another religion, let alone the following of it, as a basis for persecution.

MONITORING LOCAL UNHCR FIELD OFFICE PRACTICE

There have been numerous reports of UNHCR irregularities regarding the RSD process. The purpose of this section is to highlight some of the common concerns raised about UNHCR field office practice and to identify how you can best respond to these concerns if they arise during the course of your engagement with the UNHCR process.

Unless otherwise noted, the references in the section are to the UNHCR Procedural Standards.

Advocacy leads to greater advocacy

As you / your organisation / your church help refugees, you will discover gaps in the local protection framework or areas of procedural unfairness that should be addressed by the local UNHCR Office.

The documentation of your concerns and the identification of first-hand information to confirm the implications of these concerns is very important. Thought should be given to how you can monitor the processes and the people within the UNHCR and your local community who may be in a position to advocate about these concerns with the UNHCR office.

Each UNHCR Office should have a department whose responsibility it is to respond to complaints about the system. This is an important department for you to make contact with.

Implementation of UNHCR procedural standards[59]

Access to legal representation during interviews

In numerous field offices of the UNHCR, legal advocates are not allowed to accompany refugee applicants into RSD interviews. Without legal representatives in the RSD process, the probabilities of success for the refugee applicant are significantly lower and it will be nearly impossible to collect information necessary for reforms that benefit all refugee applicants.

The presence of legal advocates at all stages of the RSD process may be the most critical issue for the rights of refugees generally. You should encourage all those working in this field to work together to put pressure on local UNHCR field offices to allow the presence of legal advocates at RSD interviews.

As noted earlier, the UNHCR has declared that asylum seekers have a right to legal counsel "at all stages of the procedure". (UNHCR, Asylum-Processes: Fair and Efficient Asylum Procedures, para 50g, 2001). Furthermore, in its own RSD procedures, UNHCR's standards allow asylum seekers to obtain the assistance of legal representatives and advisors (section 4.3.3). Using the UNHCR Procedural Standards, NGOs should address both local offices and UNHCR offices abroad where local practice differs from UNHCR best practice.

Notification of denial of refugee status

Under Section 6.4, the UNHCR is to notify the refugee applicant of a positive or negative refugee status determination by letter. In the case of a negative decision, the UNHCR letter should give adequate information to allow the refugee applicant to know whether an appeal is appropriate and then to address all relevant facts and issues. The UNHCR has a policy of permitting field offices to use a standard form rejection letter.

A sample can be found in Appendix L below. You / your organisation should make sure that it is standard practice that all refugees receive a notice of denial of refugee status. If a pattern of non-notification persists, a formal complaint should be filed with both the head of the local UNHCR office and with the international headquarters in Geneva.

Changes in UNHCR procedural standards[60]

Access to evidence

UNHCR has advised governments that refugee applicants and decision-makers should usually be in equal positions with regard to access to evidence. This ensures that there is "equality of arms" between the applicant and the decision-maker; that is, neither party is procedurally disadvantaged. UNHCR field offices may withhold evidence only in "exceptional" cases.[61]

Unfortunately, contrary to this stated position, UNHCR practice in 80 countries takes a contradictory approach, which means that most evidence in the possession of the UNHCR office is not disclosed to the applicant.

We would encourage you to request background information that the UNHCR may possess concerning relevant country information reports on the particular country to which the applicant may be returned if refused RSD. When making a request, state the best practice provision of the UNHCR as mentioned here concerning access to information.

Access to interview transcripts

Under Section 2.1.2, the UNHCR will allow the interview transcript to be read back to the refugee applicant but will not disclose interview transcripts and notes to the applicant. Indeed, UNHCR, as a general rule, withholds "documents generated by UNHCR or a source other than the individual concerned" (2.1.2). The UNHCR states that security concerns govern such restrictions on evidence.

UNHCR does, however, allow provision of certain "documents generated by UNHCR" in the following circumstances:

- disclosure is for a legitimate purpose
- disclosure will not jeopardize the security of the applicant, their family members or those affiliated closely with them

While legal advocates can create a rough transcript, such records are not a substitute for a comprehensive verbatim record of the transcript.

Given the use to which the transcript is put by UNHCR in decision-making, disclosure of the interview transcript to the applicant is clearly in the interests of equality of arms between the decision-maker and the applicant. So the transcript should be made available to the refugee applicant for appeal. The burden of producing such a transcript is minor compared to the potential harm the refugee applicant might experience when returned to a potentially hostile environment. We would encourage you to make requests for disclosure of the interview transcript and challenge the UNHCR's position on this at the highest level.

Adequate reasons for denial of refugee status[62]

Whilst the UNHCR permits the use of a set format letter rather than a personalised letter to inform of a denial of refugee status, the UNHCR has stated to its field staff that "best practice" requires the provision of specific facts or an explanation as to why the application was rejected.

Present practice among field offices varies as to the level of information provided. It is important to monitor the level of information provided. If the letter of refusal does not explain why the evidence was not deemed credible or why the applicant did not meet one of the specified grounds you are encouraged to request a more detailed explanation from the UNHCR office.

Furthermore, it is "best practice" for UNHCR to provide sufficient detail to enable the applicant to know why the evidence relied upon was deemed to be insufficient and a summary of why the evidence was rejected.

Separate appeal body[63]

UNHCR recognizes the right of rejected refugee applicants to make an appeal. Under 7.1.1, the appeal should be heard by an eligibility officer other than the officer who heard the claim in the first instance. UNHCR in its RSD appeals is only partially compliant with the international standards regarding appeals of administrative proceedings. In a 2001 document, "Asylum-Processes: Fair and Efficient Asylum Procedures", appeals are considered to be a "key procedural safeguard", yet UNHCR lacks a separate, independent entity for re-evaluating the initial refugee determination. Owing to the gravity of the decision delegated to UNHCR in RSD, there should be an independent appellate body to serve as a check and balance on the initial RSD decision. Many large organisations are involved in petitioning for change in this matter.

At the local level you can seek to ensure that a different officer determines the appeal from the one who assessed the first instance application.

Record any concerns you may have about the appeal process and raise them at the local office and with any of the individuals you have identified in your country who are engaged in the care and protection of refugees.

Mandatory appellate interview[64]

If a refugee applicant files an appeal, it should be mandatory that they receive a separate interview. An appellate interview should be less time-consuming, as the issues are much narrower than those in the initial RSD interview. This appeal would satisfy some best practices advocated in UNHCR RSD standards, for instance, under Section 6.4.

Converts added to vulnerable applicants with UNHCR

UNHCR has accelerated procedures for identifying refugees with special needs. UNHCR has a policy of identifying vulnerable applicants at registration. UNHCR RSD standards (3.4.1 and 4.6.3) identify the following categories of special needs:

- Persons with urgent protection needs in the host country
- Victims of torture and persons suffering from trauma
- Women with special needs or who are at risk in the host country

- Child applicants (18 years and under)
- Elderly asylum seekers without support in host country
- Disabled asylum seekers without necessary support
- Asylum seekers with urgent medical needs

Converts to another religion who may be persecuted in their country of origin as a result of their conversion should be added to this list of vunerable applicants.

Other suggestions for fairer RSD procedures specific to the vulnerable position of converts to Christianity who are seeking refugee determination

More Christian translators for RSD

An ongoing concern is the impartiality of translators towards the situation of a refugee who has converted to Christianity and therefore is at risk of persecution in the home country.

You may be able to encourage translators from within the Christian community to qualify with the local UNHCR Office to serve as RSD translators. Naturally all translators should comply with the procedures prescribed by the UNHCR regarding disclosure of any conflicts of interest that might arise with each particular case. It could be argued that a Christian translator who does not disclose their religion when translating for a Christian refugee applicant could be guilty of a conflict of interest that may have civil/criminal penalties.

Panel of religious experts

One of the factors that the UNHCR and many government agencies have identified as necessary is an expert understanding of how to assess the credibility of an individual's conversion. A suggestion that should be made to the local UNHCR Office is the creation of an expert panel that can assist UNHCR in understanding how to test the credibility of an individual's conversion.

APPENDICES

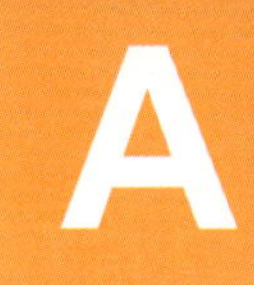

Appendix A – Sample Intake Form

APPLICANT INFORMATION

Name of Applicant:	UNHCR ID:
Sex: ☐ Male ☐ Female ☐ Other	Alternate ID:
Country of Origin:	Phone:
Unaccompanied minor: ☐ Yes: ☐ No	E-mail:
Marital Status:	Language/Dialect:
Religion:	Interpreter: ☐ Yes: ☐ No

Stage of RSD:	
Date of First Registration:	Date of Second Registration:

First Instance:	Scheduled Date:	Actual Date:
Result:	Result:	Date of Result:
Appeal:	Date of Notification:	Date Submitted:
	Result:	Date of Result:
Re-Opening:	Date Submitted:	Interview:
	Result:	Date of Result:
Other:	Date Submitted:	Interview:
	Result:	Date of Result:

Primary Case Officer:	Date assigned:

FILE INFORMATION

Date Opened:	Opened By:
Date of Birth & Age:	Any other Nationalities: ☐ Yes: ☐ No
Place of Birth:	Dependents:
Education:	
Occupation:	Travel Time:

☐ **Intake Interview Complete (see attached "summary of intake")**

Level of service:

☐ Screening only ☐ Basic counselling ☐ RSD interview prep
☐ Testimony ☐ Full Other: _______________

Communications with Applicant and Action Undertaken			
Date	Comments	Time Spent	Advisor

Date Closed:	Closed By:

Adapted from a form created by Asylum Access

Appendix B – Preliminary Registration Agreement

This is the type of form that you could adopt if you are working as an organisation. The registration agreement sets out the understanding between the asylum applicant and you as an organisation and the basis upon which you will provide assistance during the RSD application process.

I, the undersigned ______________________________
(applicant passport number, alternate ID number ____________________)

1. I understand that ________________(organisation) makes its assessment as to whether I meet the refugee definition as established by the 1951 Refugee Convention based on its understanding of how the law governs such applications.

2. If ________________(organisation) decides that my application is one which should be considered by UNHCR, ________________(organisation) will assist me in the preparation of my case including the preparation and writing of my statement of my case and the provision of legal advice about my case and assistance before and during the RSD interview and any subsequent appeal.

3. If ________________(organisation) agrees to adopt my case for RSD I will sign the Legal Agreement, which will nullify the Preliminary Agreement Registration and regulate the conditions for the provision of legal assistance by the organisation ________________. This will be processed at my first appointment.

4. Should ________________(organisation) decide they cannot provide legal advice, one of the volunteer advisers will provide me with guidance on what are my rights in the first RSD interview, if applicable, or what are my rights in the appeal process and how an application for appeal should be drafted.

5. I will be contacted by ________________(organisation) within the next ___ days to confirm whether ________________(organisation) will assist me in my application for RSD and to be told about the time of my first appointment with the organisation advisors.

If it is impossible to make contact with me on the phone number or I do not respond to messages left by the organisation within five working days or if I fail to attend any appointments without a satisfactory explanation, the organisation has the right to refuse to assist me with my application for RSD.

Name of Applicant ____________________

Phone ______________________________
Address____
____
____

Printed Name of Applicant	Signature of Applicant	Date

Advisor Name	Signature	Date

Form created by Asylum Access

Appendix C – General Confidentiality Waiver ("Waiver")

I, the undersigned _______________ (name), with UNHCR ID ______, authorize _________________________ (organisation) to act on my behalf in seeking international protection from forcible return to my country of origin.

I authorize ____________________ (organisation) to release confidential information in relation to, and in connection with, my claim for international protection, to the UNHCR.

______________________ (organisation) will not disclose other confidential information about me to other organisations or individuals without my further consent.

I have had this Authority read and if applicable, translated to me, and I understand and agree with its terms.

Printed Name of Applicant	Signature of Applicant	Date

INTERPRETER CERTIFICATION

I certify that I have honestly and accurately translated the content of this Agreement into the following language for the applicant named above: _________________________.

Printed Name of Interpreter	Signature	Date

Appendix D – Specific Confidentiality Waiver ("Waiver")

I, the undersigned ______________________________ (name), with UNHCR ID __________, authorize ________________________ (organisation) to release and/or receive confidential information in relation to, and in connection with, my claim for international protection, to the organisations and/or individuals listed below.

____

____

____

____

____

____

____

____

I have had this Agreement read and if applicable, translated to me, and I understand and agree with its terms.

Printed Name of Applicant	Signature of Applicant	Date

INTERPRETER CERTIFICATION

I certify that I have honestly and accurately translated the content of this Agreement into the following language for the applicant named above: _________________.

Printed Name of Interpreter	Signature	Date

Appendix E – Sample UNHCR Authorization

Re: Authorization To Act As Legal Representative

To be completed by the applicant

Name of Applicant:	
UNHCR Registration No.:	
Date of Notification:	

This is to certify that ______________________________ (organisation) is acting as my legal representative for all matters relating to my application for refugee status with the United Nations High Commissioner for Refugees.

I hereby authorize UNHCR to disclose to the above-named individual information or documents that I have provided directly to UNHCR, and to inform the above-named organisation of decisions taken by UNHCR regarding my application for refugee status.

This authorization is valid until a final determination in my refugee claim has been made by UNHCR, or the date upon which I give notice to UNHCR that the organisation named above is no longer authorized to act as my legal representative.

Signature of Applicant	Date

Form created by Asylum Access

Appendix F – Sample First Intake Checklist

Make sure you have done the following before the applicant leaves after first intake meeting:

- ☐ Explain to applicant the role of your legal aid organisation, and the separate role of UNHCR
- ☐ Provide applicant with the refugee definition under local and international law
- ☐ Walk applicant through RSD process if applicant is unfamiliar with the process, and clear up confusion and misunderstandings if they exist
- ☐ Complete intake form with all relevant and obtainable applicant information
- ☐ Identify basic needs of the applicant
- ☐ Health and safety questions:
    - o Do you currently have a place to live and enough to eat?
    - o Have you experienced or are you currently experiencing threats or abuse from any public authority or private person?
    - o Do you have a job?
    - o Are your children in school?
- ☐ Have applicant sign confidentiality waiver if applicable
- ☐ Explain representation agreement, and have applicant sign
- ☐ Copy and save physical and electronic copy of applicant's identity document and any other relevant documentation (passport, communications to/from UNHCR or LRO, birth certificate, marriage certificate, etc.)
- ☐ If applicant is not currently in possession of necessary documents, request that applicant return with those documents
- ☐ Provide applicant with any relevant referral information (UNHCR, HIAS, local aid and service providers, etc.)
- ☐ Set plan for follow up (make sure you have a way to contact the applicant and that they know how to contact you in case of changes)

Appendix G – Sample UNHCR RSD Application Form

Source: RSD Procedural Standards Annex 3-1:

UNHCR The UN Refugee Agency

space for **Photograph**

A photo of the applicant will normally be appended to the RSD Application Form.

UNHCR Office:	☐ Principal Applicant ☐ Derivative Status	
RSD File#:	**Reg. #:**	
Arrival Date (dd/mm/yyyy): __/__/____	**Reg. Date** (dd/mm/yyyy): __/__/____	**Special Needs:**
Reg. Staff:	**Interpreter:**	
Linked RSD Files:		

Registration Information Sheet	
Parts A to H must be completed for every adult and child Applicant, including family members and other dependants who are accompanying a Principal Applicant.	
Part A – Basic Bio Data	
1. Full Name (Underline main name): 2. Other Names used:	
3. Father's Name:	4. Mother's Name:
5. Sex: ☐ Male ☐ Female	6. Nationality:
7. Date of Birth (dd/mm/yyyy): __/__/____ (If not known give estimated year of birth):	
8. Place of Birth:	
9. Marital Status: ☐ Single ☐ Married ☐ Engaged ☐ Separated ☐ Divorced ☐ Widowed	
10. Spouse's Name (if applicable):	
11. Religion:	12. Ethnicity:
13. Full Address of Last Place of Residence in Home Country:	
14. Present Address & Contact Numbers:	

Part B – Education (Highest Level)				
Name of Institution	Place/Country	From (mm/yyyy)	To (mm/yyyy)	Qualification Obtained
		__/__/____	__/__/____	
		__/__/____	__/__/____	

Part C – Occupation (Most recent in the home country)				
Name of Employer	Place/Country	From (mm/yyyy)	To (mm/yyyy)	Job Title
		__/__/____	__/__/____	
		__/__/____	__/__/____	

Part D – Identification Documents / Other Documents Provided				
Document type / Number	Place of issue	Date of issue (dd/mm/yyyy)	Date of expiry (dd/mm/yyyy)	Original provided?
		__/__/____	__/__/____	☐ Yes ☐ No
		__/__/____	__/__/____	☐ Yes ☐ No
		__/__/____	__/__/____	☐ Yes ☐ No
		__/__/____	__/__/____	☐ Yes ☐ No
		__/__/____	__/__/____	☐ Yes ☐ No
		__/__/____	__/__/____	☐ Yes ☐ No
		__/__/____	__/__/____	☐ Yes ☐ No

Documents obtained illegally:
If any of the documents listed above were not issued legally, please explain how they were obtained.

Missing Documents:
If you are missing identity documents or other documents that are relevant to your claim, please explain why you do not have these documents.

If you are missing documents will you be able to obtain these documents in the future? If not, please explain why.

Part E – Applicant's UNHCR Registration History		
1. Have you already been registered by UNHCR? ☐ Yes ☐ No		
If **yes,** where were you registered?	Registration #	Date of registration: (dd / mm / yyyy) __/__/____
2. Have you ever applied for refugee protection with UNHCR or a Government? ☐ Yes ☐ No If **yes**		
Where?	When?	Decision and / or status obtained:

FAMILY / HOUSEHOLD COMPOSITION

If this Applicant is applying as a dependent family member of a principal applicant, and the information in Parts F to H is identical to the form of the principal applicant, the registration number of the principal applicant may be provided instead of completing Parts F to H.

Registration No of Principal Applicant____

Part F – Family Members and Dependants accompanying the Applicant

Full Name	Individual registration #	Relationship to applicant	Sex (M/f)	Date of birth (dd/mm/yyyy)
				__/__/____
				__/__/____
				__/__/____
				__/__/____
				__/__/____
				__/__/____
				__/__/____
				__/__/____
				__/__/____
				__/__/____

Part G – Close Family Members and Dependents in Home Country

Full Name	Relationship to applicant	Date of birth (dd/mm/yyyy)	Citizenship	Occupation
		__/__/____		
		__/__/____		
		__/__/____		
		__/__/____		
		__/__/____		
		__/__/____		

Part H – Non-Accompanying Family Members and Dependents Living Outside Home Country

Full Name	Relationship to applicant	Date of birth (dd/mm/yyyy)	Address	Status there	Citizenship
		__/__/____			
		__/__/____			
		__/__/____			
		__/__/____			
		__/__/____			

Additional Information for Mandate RSD			
Parts I to K must be completed for every Adult Applicant, by children who are applying as Principal Applicants and every unaccompanied or separated child.			
Part I – Details of Travel			
1. Date of Departure from Home Country (dd/mm/yyyy): _ _/_ _ /_ _ _ _			
2. Means of Travel out of Home Country:			
3. Exit Point from Home Country:			
4. Countries of Transit:	Period		Travel Document Used
	From (mm/dd/yyyy)	To (mm/dd/yyyy)	
	_ _/_ _ /_ _ _ _	_ _/_ _ /_ _ _ _	
	_ _/_ _ /_ _ _ _	_ _/_ _ /_ _ _ _	
	_ _/_ _ /_ _ _ _	_ _/_ _ /_ _ _ _	
	_ _/_ _ /_ _ _ _	_ _/_ _ /_ _ _ _	
5. Entry point in Host Country:			
6. Date of arrival in Host Country (dd/mm/yyyy): _ _/_ _ /_ _ _ _			
7. Have you been to Host Country before? ☐ Yes ☐ No If **yes**, please provide date and duration of stay:			
Part J – Sex of Interviewer / Language(s) of Interview			
Do you have a preference to be interviewed by a staff member and interpreter of a particular sex? ☐ Yes ☐ No If **yes**, indicate which sex: ☐ Male ☐ Female What language(s) do you prefer for UNHCR interviews? ______________________________			
Part K – Written Statement			
When answering the questions below, you should tell us everything about why you believe that you are in need of refugee protection. You should provide as much detail as possible, including the date the relevant events occurred. It is important that you provide full and truthful answers to these questions. If you need more space, please attach a page(s) with the details.			

1. Why did you leave your home country?

2. What do you believe may happen to you, or members of your household, if you return to your home country? Please explain why.

Declaration
To be signed by the Applicant

I declare the information I have supplied on and with this form is complete, correct and current in every detail.

I understand that if I have given false or misleading information, my application for refugee status may be refused, or, if I have been recognized as a refugee, the recognition may be cancelled.

I undertake to inform UNHCR of any significant changes to my circumstances while my application is being considered, including any changes to my address and contact numbers, the arrival or departure of members of my household or other changes in the composition of my household.

Signature of Applicant:____________________

Date:____________________

Place:____________________

Appendix H – UNHCR Asylum Seeker Certificate

UNITED NATIONS	NATIONS UNIES
HIGH COMMISSIONER	HAUT COMMISSARIAT
FOR REFUGEES	POUR LES REFUGIES

Insert Address Details for UN Field Office issuing the certificate.

Insert Photo Here

Reference No:

Asylum Seeker Certificate

Full Name:	
Date of Birth:	
Nationality:	
Issued On:	
Valid Until:	
Passport Number:	

This is to certify that the above mentioned person is an asylum seeker whose claim for refugee status is being examined by the Office of the High Commissioner for Refugees. As an asylum seeker he/she should in particular be protected from forcible return to a country where he/she claims to face threats to his/her life or freedom, pending a final decision on his/her refugee status. Any assistance accorded to the above mentioned individual and family members (if any) would be appreciated.

Details and photographs of family members (if any) are enclosed below. Should you have any questions regarding the asylum seeker(s) please contact the UNHCR Office in (address details would be specified here).

Signed.....................................

UNHCR Liaison Officer

I

Appendix I – Self-Help Kit RSD Application

Self-Help Kit

How to Write Your Statement for Your Refugee Status Determination ("RSD") Interview with UNHCR

July 2008

Self-Help Kit
How to write your statement for your RSD interview with UNHCR

YOUR RSD INTERVIEW WITH UNHCR

The purpose of your RSD interview with UNHCR is for UNHCR to determine whether you meet the definition of a refugee under the 1951 Convention Relating to the Status of Refugees.[65] To meet this definition you must meet all of the following criteria:[66]

1. You must be outside the country you are from; and
2. You must be unable or unwilling to return to the country you are from;
3. Because you have a well-founded fear:
    a. You must be afraid; and
    b. There must be objective evidence from your country (e.g. newspaper articles, NGO reports, UN reports) that shows you have a good reason to be afraid;
4. That if you return to your country, you will be persecuted (e.g. there is a threat to your life, freedom, or other human rights);
5. Based on one or more of the following reasons:
    a. Your race;
    b. Your religion;
    c. Your nationality;
    d. Your political opinion; or
    e. Your membership of a particular social group (this could be your family or persons with similar backgrounds, habits or social status, often with a characteristic which is innate, unchangeable or fundamental).

At your RSD interview, a UNHCR officer will ask you to talk about your background, what happened to you in your country to make you leave and why you can't go back to your country, so that UNHCR can work out whether you meet all of the criteria in the refugee definition.

WHAT IS THE PURPOSE OF YOUR STATEMENT?

The purpose of your statement is to tell UNHCR what happened to you in your country to make you leave and why you can't go back to your country, and by doing that, show UNHCR how you meet each of the criteria in the refugee definition.

UNHCR will use the information in your statement to ask you questions at your interview and then will use your statement, the answers that you give at your interview and information from your country to decide whether you meet the criteria in the refugee definition.

So, before writing your statement make sure you understand the definition of a refugee because understanding the definition will help you to decide what information you need to include in your statement. You should also have a look at Annex 1 of this Self Help Kit, which explains the UNHCR RSD process, and read the 'Information for Asylum Seekers' booklet that was given to you by UNHCR because it has a lot of important information about the refugee definition and your interview.

WHAT IS THE PURPOSE OF THIS SELF-HELP KIT?

This Self Help Kit will help you understand what information you should try to include in your statement and will give you an example of how to set out that information so you can make it easier for UNHCR to understand how you meet the definition of a refugee.

If you have previously submitted a statement to UNHCR, which does not cover all the information listed in this Self Help Kit, then it is fine to submit another more detailed statement covering the additional information you want UNHCR to know.

THINGS TO REMEMBER WHEN WRITING YOUR STATEMENT

When you write your statement, remember that it should:

- Include complete and truthful information about:
  - ☐ All the things that happened to you to make you leave your country;
  - ☐ Why those things happened to you and who did them;
  - ☐ How you left your country;
  - ☐ Why you can't go back to your country and what you think will happen to you if you go back.
- Explain the things that happened to you in the order they happened.
- Include as much detail as you can remember about the important things that happened and generally include the following:
  - ☐ **Dates and Times**: When things happened. For example, "On 16 June 2005 at about 6pm…". If you don't remember exact dates and times, then you should try to remember approximate dates and times or things that happened around the same time. For example, you could say something like, "One day in March 2006, late at night…", "One day, about two weeks before New Year in 2007, early in the morning…", "Soon after my 30th birthday…", "When I was about 20 years old…", or "During the summer of 2006…". You can also say things like "Soon after the [last event]…" or "Around the same time as the [last event]…".
  - ☐ **Places:** Where things happened. If you can't remember the exact place, then you should try to give as much detail as possible or try to describe what the place was like. For example, you could say, "I was kidnapped when I was walking from Town A to Town B", "I went to a large brick house which was about 5 minutes walk from my house" or "I was taken to a small village about 30km south of my village".
  - ☐ **People:** If you can remember the names of people, you should always include this information. If you don't know people's names or you can't remember them, then try to describe the people, especially if you're scared of them, they're people who hurt you, they're the reason why you left your country or if you think they're important to what happened to you. When describing people, you can explain what they were wearing,

whether they had weapons, what language they spoke, etc. You should also explain who you think the people were and why you think that.

☐ **Duration:** When you're describing things that happened to you, include how long these things lasted. For example, you could say, "I was kept in prison for two days" or "I was in the hospital for two weeks".

Some other things you need to remember when writing your statement:

- Your statement should be in your own words and must only include information that is true and that is not exaggerated.
- If you can write in your own language then you should write your statement.
- If you cannot write in your own language, make sure that the person who writes the statement for you only includes information you have told them to include.
- Don't let anyone tell you what to include in your statement or let anyone add anything to your statement that you disagree with or is untrue.
- You should try to keep your statement to less than 10 pages especially if your statement is not in English because if it is longer it will take UNHCR more time to translate it.
- If there are things you don't remember, don't make something up. It is fine to say that you don't remember.
- If there is something you are not sure about then you should say something like, "I believe that ..." or "I think that ..." but don't say, "I know that..." Also explain why you are not sure.
- Your statement should be consistent with all information that you have previously told or given to UNHCR. If you plan to include information in your statement that is not consistent with information that you have previously told or given to UNHCR, then explain the inconsistencies in your statement.
- If you plan to include new information in your statement, explain why you did not previously tell UNHCR about this information.

WHAT TO INCLUDE IN YOUR STATEMENT

One way you can organize your statement is set out in sections 1 to 8 below.[67] Remember this is only an example and you don't have to set out your statement in the same way. What is important is that you tell UNHCR the truth about what happened to you in your country to make you leave and why you can't go back so that UNHCR can work out whether you meet the definition of a refugee.

Section 1: UNHCR address and personal information

Write the date, UNHCR's address and address the letter to UNHCR. Then, introduce yourself and say that this is your statement for your RSD interview with UNHCR.

Then, write your UNHCR ID, gender, nationality, ethnicity, date of birth, place of birth, the languages that you speak fluently, passport country and number (if you have one), marital status, the date you arrived in this country, the date you registered with UNHCR, the date of your RSD interview with UNHCR and your current contact information.[68]

Section 2: Background information

In a section called "Background Information" give UNHCR some brief information about you and your family. This section should not be longer than 5 to 10 lines. You should include very brief information about who is in your family, where you grew up and where you and your family lived before you came to this country. You should also tell UNHCR whether your family is with you in this country and if not, where they're now living.

Section 3: What happened to make you leave your country?

In a section called "What Happened to Make Me Leave My Country" write about all of the problems you had that made you leave your country. Remember what you're trying to do in this section is show UNHCR how you meet the refugee definition and specifically, why you have a 'well founded fear of persecution' because of one or more of the following: your race, religion, nationality, political opinion or membership of a social group.

Make sure you:

- Write about the problems you had in the order they happened. If other people in your family had similar problems before your problems started, then first write about their problems. End this section with the last problem that happened to make you leave your country.
- Include details of when and where you had the problems, who was involved (or who you think was involved and why you think that) and what they said and did.
- Explain how the problems made you feel and what you were worried or scared about.
- Explain why you think these problems happened to you.
- If you know of other people who have also had similar problems to yours, include brief information about those other people and what happened to them. Explain how you know this information.
- If you have committed a serious crime in a country other than this one, explain what you did, where and when you did it and why you did it.

Section 4: Why did you have to leave your country and how did you leave?

In a section called "Why I Had to Leave My Country and How I Left":

- Explain why you thought you had to leave your country and what you thought would happen to you if you stayed any longer in your country.
- If you left your country in the past but had to come back to your country then explain what happened. Also explain if you tried to leave your country but couldn't and what stopped you.
- Explain what you did to leave your country and who helped you.

If you came straight here from your country and registered with the UNHCR quite soon after, then include a paragraph similar to the following:

> I left [*insert city, your country*] on [*date, month, year*] and came to this country on [*date, month, year*]. I traveled by [*insert the type(s) of transport you took to get here*]. I registered with UNHCR on [*date, month, year*].

If you passed through other countries before coming here, then explain which countries you went to, how long you stayed and whether you tried to get help in those countries. Similarly, if you waited more than one month after arriving in this country to register with UNHCR, explain why.

Section 5: Why can't you go back to your country?

In a section called "Why I Can't Go Back to My Country" explain:

- Whether you did anything to stop the problems that happened to you in your country and whether what you did helped. Did you try to get help from your government, the police or anyone else? When? What did they say and do? Did they help? Did you try to move to another part of your country to avoid your problems? Where did you move to and when? Did that help?

- What you think will happen to you if you return to your country and what you're scared about. Include information about who you think will hurt you and what you think they will do to you and also explain why you think those things will happen to you.

- If anyone in your country has received threats about you or had problems because of you after you left your country include this information as well.

Section 6: Conditions in this country

If there is any information about your security or your medical, physical or psychological situation that you have not already told UNHCR, then you can include that information in a section called "My Situation in --". Make sure this section is no longer than about 5 lines.

Section 7: Documents

Do you have documents that support the things that you have said in your statement? For example, do you have a passport, ID cards, medical records, membership cards for groups/organisations that you belonged to, threatening letters, letters that you have written asking for help, responses to your letters, police reports etc.? If so, then list the names of each of these documents in a section called "Documents" at the end of your statement.

Section 8: Signature

Finally, sign your statement. You can also thank UNHCR for considering your application and say that the information you have included is the truth.

SAMPLE STATEMENT

Your final statement could look something like the example below.

Date: [*insert the date that you're writing the letter*]

United Nations High Commissioner for Refugees

Attention: RSD Unit

Dear Sir/Madam,

My name is [*insert your name*] and this is my statement for my RSD interview with UNHCR.

NI Number: [*insert NI number*]
Gender: [*insert whether you're male or female*]
Nationality: [*insert your nationality*]
Ethnicity: [*insert your ethnicity*]
Languages: [*insert the languages that you can speak and understand fluently*]
Date of Birth: [*insert your date of birth*]
Place of Birth: [*insert the city and the country where you were born*]
Passport Country and Number: [*include your passport country ID number*]
Marital status: [*state whether you're married, single or widowed*]
Date arrived in this country: [*insert date*]
Date registered with UNHCR: [*insert date*]
Date of RSD interview with UNHCR: [*insert date*]
Current contact information: [*insert your mobile number if you have one, otherwise your address*]

Background Information

[*Insert your information]*

What Happened to Make Me Leave My Country

[*Insert your information]*

Why I Had to Leave My Country and How I Left My Country

[*Insert your information]*

Why I Can't Go Back to My Country

[*Insert your information]*

My Situation in This Country

[*Insert your information]*

My Documents

[*Insert your information]*

All the information that I have included in this statement is true. Thank you for considering my application for refugee status.

[*Sign your name here*]

____

[*Write your name here*]

BEFORE YOU GIVE YOUR STATEMENT TO UNHCR

Before you give your statement to UNHCR:

- Reread the statement to make sure that you have included everything you wanted to include in the statement to help UNHCR decide whether you meet the definition of a refugee.
- Make sure that everything you have included is the truth and has not been exaggerated.
- Make sure your statement is written in the order that things happened and makes sense.
- Check whether anything in the statement is different to what you have said in your registration interview with UNHCR or any other information that you have given or told to UNHCR. If there is anything that is different, then explain why it's different.
- Make sure you take a copy of the statement for yourself so that you can use it to prepare for your interview. Remember that UNCHR will likely use your statement to ask you questions at your RSD interview.

WHEN YOU GIVE YOUR STATEMENT TO UNHCR

- Try to give your statement to UNCHR at least one month before the scheduled date of your RSD interview with UNHCR.
- If the documents that you have listed in your statement have not previously been given to UNHCR, then also give UNHCR <u>copies</u> of these documents at the same time that you give the statement to UNHCR. <u>Do not</u> give any original documents to UNCHR.

Form provided by Asylum Access

Appendix J – Sample Mock Interview Questions

1. Have you ever been to (host country) before?
2. When was your first entry to (host country)?
3. For how many years have you lived in (host country)?
4. What was the last city of residence in your home country and how long did you live there?
5. What did you do for a living in your home country?
6. How was your economic situation in your home country?
7. How would you describe the place where you lived, and what was your situation like there?
8. Did you ever have problems with anyone?
9. Did you ever receive threats? What kind? From whom?
10. How many threats did you receive?
11. How frequently did you receive threats?
12. How long after the threats did you leave your home country?
13. Did you go to the police in your home country?
14. Why did you decide to leave your country?
15. How did you leave your country?
16. Why did you decide to come to (host country)?
17. With whom did you enter (host country)?
18. With whom do you live in (host country)?
19. Have you returned to your country since you left?
20. How did you find out about the option to apply for refugee status?
21. Why didn't you apply for refugee status sooner?
22. What would you do if your application for refugee status is denied?
23. What would you do if you were granted refugee status?
24. Would you like to add anything else to the interview?

Certificate provided in Annex 3-1 of UNHCR Procedural Standards for RSD under UNHCR's Mandate

Appendix K – Sample UNHCR Refugee Certificate

UNITED NATIONS
HIGH COMMISSIONER
FOR REFUGEES

NATIONS UNIES
HAUT COMMISSARIAT
POUR LES REFUGIES

Insert Address of Country Office

Reference Number: Date of Issue:

UNHCR REFUGEE CERTIFICATE

Name of Applicant:
UNHCR Registration No:
Date of birth:
Place of birth:
Nationality:

Insert Photo Here

TO WHOM IT MAY CONCERN

This is to certify that the above-named person has been recognised as a refugee by the United Nations High Commissioner for Refugees, pursuant to its mandate.

As a refugee _______________________________ [INSERT NAME HERE] is a person of concern to the Office of the United Nations High Commissioner for Refugees, and should, in particular, be protected from forcible return to a country where _______________________________ [INSERT NAME HERE] would face threats to his or her life or freedom. Any assistance accorded to the above-named individual would be most appreciated.

Questions regarding the information contained in this document may be directed to the United Nations High Commissioner for Refugees at the address above.

(Signature of designated UNHCR Officer)

This document is only valid in the original when bearing official UNHCR stamp

Appendix L – Sample Notification of Negative RSD Decision

UNITED NATIONS
HIGH COMMISSIONER
FOR REFUGEES

NATIONS UNIES
HAUT COMMISSARIAT
POUR LES REFUGIES

UNHCR
The UN Refugee Agency

Insert Address of Country Office

Name of Applicant:	
UNHCR Registration No:	
Date of Notification:	

Notification of Negative RSD Decision

Dear [Name of Applicant]:

We regret to inform you that after a thorough assessment of your refugee claim and careful consideration of all available information UNHCR has determined that you are not eligible for international refugee protection under UNHCR's mandate. The decision that you are not eligible for international refugee protection has been based on the following determinations.

Select each paragraph that has been determined to apply to the Applicant. As a best practice after each ticked paragraph provide a brief explanation of the specific facts in the Applicant's claim that were relied upon to reach the conclusion stated in the relevant paragraph. Paragraphs that are not relevant to the reasons for the decision should be deleted.

Eligibility Officers should be guided by the factors set out in the RSD Procedural Standards §6.2 notifying Applicants of negative RSD Decisions to determine whether it is necessary and appropriate to permit disclosure of certain types of information.

☐ You are not outside of your country of origin and are therefore not eligible for refugee status.

☐ You have more than one nationality and have not established that you are unable to obtain effective protection in all of the countries of which you are a national

☐ You are not considered to be in need of refugee protection because you now have rights and obligations in the country in which you have taken up residence that are the same as the rights enjoyed by persons who are nationals of that country.

☐ The reasons you have provided for being unwilling or unable to return to your country of origin are not related to the criteria for refugee status under the UNHCR's mandate.

☐ The information you provided in support of your claim was not sufficiently detailed and you did not provide a reasonable explanation for failing to provide information that was relevant to your claim.

☐ The information you provided to UNHCR was not considered to be reliable on points that are material to your claim, for the following reasons:

Substantial inconsistencies were found within the information you provided referring to your claim.

Substantial inconsistencies were found between the information you provided and available sources of information about your country of origin.

The information you provided was not believable or convincing.

☐ The harm you fear is not of the nature and/or seriousness as to constitute a form of persecution.

☐ The authorities in your country of origin are able to provide effective protection from the harm you fear.

☐ You are able to live in another part of your country of origin without fear of persecution and could reasonably return to live in this area without undue hardship.

☐ The Officer has determined that you have committed or contributed to committing certain serious acts and are therefore excluded from international protection

If you believe that this decision has been reached because of an error, you may apply to have this decision reconsidered on appeal. To request an appeal, you must complete the attached **Appeal Application Form** and return it to the UNHCR Office within 30 days from the date on which notification of this decision was issued to you, as noted at the top of this letter.

For further information on the procedures for making an appeal with this Office *(summarise the relevant procedures in the UNHCR Office or indicate how the Applicant can obtain information about the procedures to file an Appeal).*

Appendix M – Sample Appeal Application Form

UNITED NATIONS
HIGH COMMISSIONER
FOR REFUGEES

NATIONS UNIES
HAUT COMMISSARIAT
POUR LES REFUGIES

Registration No:	
RSD File No:	
Date of notification of decision:	
Date Appeal Application Received:	

APPEAL APPLICATION FORM FOR REFUGEE STATUS DETERMINATION

In the space provided please explain why you believe that the decision reached in your refugee claim is wrong. If you claim that any of the facts relied upon by UNHCR in reaching the decision in your refugee claim are incorrect, please explain why you believe this and provide the correct facts. Provide any relevant information that was not previously presented to UNHCR, and explain why the information was not provided before. You may also indicate on the Appeal Application Form any issues or incidences relating to the procedures for processing your refugee claim that you believe affected your ability to present your claim.

Name of Applicant:____________________________________

Date of Birth:____

Reasons for Appeal

Additional sheets should be attached as needed.

Appendix N – Self-Help Kit Appeal Response

Self-Help Kit

How to Appeal UNHCR's Rejection of Your Application for Refugee Status

April 2009

Self-Help Kit
How to appeal UNHCR's rejection of your application for refugee status

Table of Contents

APPEALING A REJECTION

The purpose of the UNHCR's Refugee Status Determination ("RSD") process is to determine whether you meet the definition of a refugee under the 1951 Convention relating to the Status of Refugees ("the Convention").[69] You must convince UNHCR that you meet each of the requirements of the Convention definition of a refugee. UNHCR can only help you if you meet the definition of a refugee – the fact that you might be suffering for other reasons is not relevant to UNHCR.

UNHCR uses any statements you have given them, your RSD interview(s), and information from your home country to decide whether you meet the Convention definition of a refugee.

If UNHCR rejects your application for refugee status, you have the right to appeal.[70] The purpose of the appeal process is for UNHCR to make sure that it has understood and considered all of the facts of your case and correctly applied the Convention refugee definition to the facts of your case. Just like in your RSD application, the question in your appeal is whether you meet the Convention definition of a refugee. UNHCR can decide to accept your appeal, reject your appeal, or call you for an interview for more information before making a decision.[71]

APPEAL DEADLINE

If you wish to appeal, you must complete the "Appeal Application Form" attached to the "Notice of Reasons for Decision" and return it to UNHCR within **30 days** of the date of notification.[72]

WHAT IS THE PURPOSE OF YOUR APPEAL STATEMENT?

The aim of your appeal statement is to convince UNHCR that it made a mistake and that you are a Convention refugee. Whether you meet the definition of a refugee is the only issue that is relevant to UNHCR.

Your appeal statement should:

- respond directly to the specific reasons that UNHCR gave for rejecting your application;
- provide any new information or clarify information that UNHCR did not understand or did not consider; and
- explain how all your information shows that you meet the Convention definition of a refugee.

WHAT IS THE PURPOSE OF THIS SELF-HELP KIT?

This Self Help Kit will help you understand what information you should include in your appeal statement and give you an example of how to set out that information.

UNDERSTANDING YOUR REJECTION REASONS

UNHCR will explain why it rejected your application for refugee status in a letter entitled "Notification of Reasons for Decision" ("Notification"). These reasons will generally fall into one of these 10 categories ("Rejection Reasons"):

1. You are not outside your home country;
2. You have more than one nationality and you have not shown that none of those countries can protect you;
3. You do not need refugee protection because you have the same rights in this country as a national;
4. The reasons you gave for being afraid to return to your home country are not related to the criteria in the Convention refugee definition, namely:
    a. Your race;
    b. Your religion;
    c. Your nationality;
    d. Your political opinion; or
    e. Your membership in a particular social group (this could be your family or persons with similar backgrounds, habits or social status);
5. You did not give sufficiently detailed information to support your claim, or you did not give a reason why you could not give more detailed information;
6. UNHCR did not consider your information reliable or credible because:
    a. You gave inconsistent information (i.e. you stated different facts in your interview than in your written statement);
    b. You gave information that was inconsistent with other sources of information about your home country; or
    c. You gave information that was not believable or convincing;
7. The harm you fear is not a kind of harm or a serious enough harm to meet the Convention definition of "persecution", namely a threat to your life, freedom, or fundamental human rights;
8. The authorities in your home country can protect you;
9. You can live in another part of your home country without fear of persecution;
10. You have committed or contributed to serious criminal or similar acts that exclude you from refugee protection.

WHEN YOU SHOULD APPEAL?

UNHCR does not set down rules about the grounds on which asylum seekers can appeal. However, there are only limited circumstances in which an appeal is likely to succeed. These are if:

(1) UNHCR did not understand or consider all of the facts of your case, or

(2) UNHCR did not correctly apply the Convention refugee definition to the facts of your case.

This appeal kit does not deal with how to argue that UNHCR did not correctly apply the Convention definition of a refugee. However, the Convention definition of a refugee is explained below.

The following lists some reasons why UNHCR may not have properly considered all the facts of your case, and these can be grounds for appealing:

1. The rejection was based on credibility problems (Rejection Reasons 5-6) and the interviewer did not give you an opportunity to properly explain those issues at your RSD interview; or

2. You presented evidence that UNHCR did not adequately consider; or

3. You have new evidence to support your claim; or

4. There was a serious breach of procedural fairness, meaning that the RSD interview or process was so unfair that you could not properly present your claim. Some examples of breaches of procedural fairness include:

    a. You did not understand the process because of some problem with interpretation;

    b. You felt uncomfortable with the conduct or some characteristic of the interviewer or interpreter;

    c. You did not have an opportunity to present relevant evidence;

    d. You did not believe that your information would be kept confidential; or

    e. You were asked inappropriate questions.

UNHCR will not change its decision if you have already presented all relevant evidence, UNHCR already understands the facts of your case, and UNHCR's application of the Convention refugee definition is clearly correct.

THINGS TO REMEMBER WHEN WRITING YOUR APPEAL STATEMENT

When you write your appeal statement, remember that it should:

- Respond directly to the specific reasons that UNHCR gave for rejecting your application in the Notification.

- Be as detailed as possible about why UNHCR should reverse its decision and why you meet the Convention definition of a refugee. It is not enough to say that UNHCR was wrong or made a mistake. Rather, you should concentrate on specific problems with UNHCR's understanding of the facts. Those problems should be serious enough to cause UNHCR to reconsider its decision.

- Highlight problems related to credibility or evidence rather than problems related to procedural fairness. Before focusing on procedural problems ask yourself, "If all of these procedural problems were resolved, would there still be problems related to credibility or evidence that UNHCR identified in its Notification?" If there are no other problems, then procedural issues alone will not cause UNHCR to reverse its decision.

- Add or clarify information. Don't just repeat the information you provided in your initial RSD statement.

When you write your appeal statement, remember that:

- Your appeal statement should be in your own words and must only include information that is true and that is not exaggerated.
- If you can write in your own language then you should write your appeal statement.
- If you cannot write in your own language, make sure that the person who writes the appeal statement for you only includes information you have told them to include.
- Don't let anyone tell you what to include in your appeal statement or let anyone add anything to your appeal statement that you disagree with or that is untrue.
- You should try to keep your appeal statement to less than 10 pages, especially if it is not in English, because if it is longer it will take UNHCR more time to translate it.
- If there are things you don't remember, don't make something up. It is fine to say that you don't remember.
- If there is something you are not sure about then you should say something like, "I believe that …" or "I think that …" but don't say, "I know that …". Also explain why you are not sure.
- Your appeal statement should be consistent with all information that you have previously told or given to UNHCR. If you plan to include information in your appeal statement that is not consistent with information that you have previously told or given to UNHCR, then explain the inconsistencies in your appeal statement.
- If you plan to include new information in your appeal statement, explain why you did not previously tell UNHCR about this information (eg because you did not know about it before, or because it has only recently happened).

WHAT TO INCLUDE IN YOUR APPEAL STATEMENT

One way you can organize your appeal statement is explained here.[73] Remember, this is only an example and you don't have to organize your appeal statement this way. What is important is that you explain why UNHCR should reconsider its decision and why you meet the Convention definition of a refugee.

Section 1: UNHCR address and personal information

Write the date, UNHCR's address and address the letter to UNHCR. Then, introduce yourself and say that this is your appeal of UNHCR's rejection of your application for refugee status.

Write your UNHCR ID, gender, nationality, ethnicity, date of birth, place of birth, the languages that you speak fluently, passport country and number (if you have one), marital status, the date you arrived in this country, the date you registered with UNHCR, the date(s) of your first instance interview(s) with UNHCR, the date of notification of UNHCR's reasons for rejection, and your current contact information.

Section 2: Procedural problems with UNHCR

In this section, write about any procedural problems that you had with your UNHCR interview – meaning things that happened in your interview where the UNHCR did not treat you fairly.

For example, if you believe that your testimony was not properly translated or that the interviewer asked inappropriate questions, then explain that in this section. Then explain why you think that UNHCR made the wrong decision because of these things (for example, that UNHCR didn't understand your information properly because of misinterpretation).

Section 3: Addressing the rejection reasons

Write in detail about all of the reasons why UNHCR should not have rejected your application for refugee status. How you organize this section will depend on the reasons UNHCR gave for rejecting your application and the reasons that you have to appeal. A good way to begin to organize is:

- List each of the reasons that UNHCR gave for rejecting your appeal as a separate sub-heading within this section (include all of the reasons in your Notification, not just the ones listed in numbered or lettered paragraphs); and
- Under each sub-heading, give the specific facts and arguments to explain why you believe UNHCR was mistaken and should reconsider that particular point, focusing on the Appeal Reasons listed on above.

You should put your best arguments first. Similarly, if there is one piece of information that addresses several of UNHCR's Rejection Reasons, you should include it at the beginning.

We are not able to give detailed suggestions on arguments that you can use for every possible reason UNHCR may have rejected you. However, the list below suggests how to deal with the issues that arise most frequently. Please keep in mind that this is general information, not legal advice.

Rejection Reason 5: ***You did not give sufficiently detailed information to support your claim, or you did not give a reason why you could not give more detailed information.***

Essentially, this means that UNHCR does not think you gave enough information to convince them that your claim is true, or that you meet the Convention definition of a refugee. UNHCR should point out specific areas, or examples of areas, where it needs more information in the Notification. If you do not understand what information UNHCR needs, you should contact the UNHCR's RSD Unit and ask for clarification.

If your application is rejected for this reason, then you need to provide more information to UNHCR. UNHCR is looking for details like names, dates, times, places, what people said or did, why they said or did it, etc. You should put facts in chronological order.

You should provide as much additional information as is necessary to give UNHCR enough detail to understand your case and decide that you meet the Convention definition of a refugee. Tell UNHCR when you are providing new information, explain why you did not provide that information previously, and attach any relevant documents.

You should focus on providing details about the specific examples UNHCR pointed out in the Notification. If you think that UNHCR needs more information on an additional topic you should provide that information. However, be sure to deal with all of the issues that UNHCR listed in the Notification, even if you don't think that the information is important, or think other information is more important.

Rejection Reason 6: ***UNHCR did not consider your information reliable or "credible".***

Information is not "credible" when the interviewer believes that it is not likely that you are telling the truth. UNHCR's Notification usually says what information UNHCR did not believe and, if appropriate, what outside information UNHCR considered. If the Notification does not contain that information, you should contact the UNHCR's RSD Unit and ask for it.

UNHCR usually finds that testimony is not credible either because UNHCR found inconsistencies in prior testimony (for example, the information you gave in your interview was different than in your statement) or because the information that you provided was not consistent with other information about your home country. In other words, UNHCR bases its decisions on the objective facts contained in your application and in other sources like newspapers, UN and NGO reports, etc., and not solely on the interviewer's subjective opinion about whether you were telling the truth. So, your appeal statement should focus as much as possible on objective facts like names, dates, times, places, what people said and did, etc. It is not enough to say that the interviewer should have believed you, or that it is not fair that the interviewer did not believe you.

You should explain any inconsistencies pointed out by UNHCR with as much detail as possible. That means both:

- telling UNHCR why you believe the interviewer made a mistake in deciding that the statements were inconsistent (for example, the interviewer did not consider other facts that explain what happened, there was a problem with the interpreter, or you made a mistake); and
- giving UNHCR the correct information.

Be as detailed as you can, and put information in chronological order wherever possible.

Reference the specific paragraphs, pages or documents from your prior documents where the facts in question are discussed.

You should provide as much additional information as is necessary to answer UNHCR's questions and explain why some of your information seems to be inconsistent. Tell UNHCR when you are providing new information, explain why you did not provide that information previously, and attach any new relevant documents.

Rejection Reason 7: ***The harm you fear is not a kind of harm or a serious enough harm to meet the Convention definition of "persecution".***

The Convention definition of "persecution" means a threat to your life, freedom, or other fundamental human rights. Examples of persecution include:

- death;
- torture;
- rape;
- slavery;
- arbitrary arrest or detention;
- deprivation of legal personality or citizenship; or
- deprivation of freedom of thought, conscience, or religion.

Serious economic hardship is not, however, "persecution" under the Convention unless it results from persecution on a Convention ground.

Your appeal statement should make clear why the harm you fear falls into one of these categories. You should highlight all the information that you provided showing that your life, freedom or other fundamental human rights are being threatened. You should include any new information that shows that you, your family, or others sharing similar characteristics to you and your family continue to be persecuted in your home country. Be sure to tell UNHCR when you are providing new information, and explain why you did not provide that information before.

Just as importantly, your appeal statement should explain why you fear that you will be persecuted if you return home now. In other words, you should show why your situation, and the threats that you face, are as bad or worse today as they were when you left the country.

Rejection Reason 8: ***The authorities in your home country can protect you.***

If you told UNHCR that you are afraid of persecution by non-government forces (a rebel group, family members, etc.), UNHCR may believe that the police, army, or other government authorities in your home country will protect you.

If you did seek protection from government authorities in your home country, you should explain when, where, from whom, and why you sought protection, and what happened. If you did not seek protection, you should explain why not. If you know of other people in similar circumstances who sought protection for government authorities in your home country, you can explain what happened to them.

Even if you have told UNHCR that you are afraid of persecution by government authorities, UNHCR may still believe that the police, army, or other government authorities in your home country will protect you, or at least not find you and/or persecute you.

If you believe that government authorities in your home country will find you and persecute you, you should explain why you believe this. You can use examples from your past as well as examples where government authorities have pursued your family members and/or other people in similar circumstances.

If applicable, be sure to reference the specific paragraphs, pages or documents from your prior submissions where this information is discussed. Also tell UNHCR when you are providing new information, and explain why you did not provide that information before.

Rejection Reason 9: ***You can live in another part of your home country without fear of persecution.***

UNHCR may have decided that you have a well-founded fear of persecution in one area of your home country, but not another. UNHCR cannot, however, find that you can go to this other area unless it is practically, safely, and legally accessible and livable for you, such that you could reasonably be expected to move there without undue hardship. This other area will usually be specifically identified by UNHCR in the Notification.

Your appeal statement should explain why you would have a well-founded fear of persecution in this other area, why this other area would not be accessible or livable for you, and/or why moving there would cause undue hardship. Regarding well-founded fear, explain your fear about living in this other area in the same way that you did about your home area. Regarding accessibility, livability, and undue hardship, highlight any difficulties in getting to or staying in this other area (for example, a war zone between your home area and this other area, different majority languages or ethnic groups and discrimination in this other area, etc.).

Be as detailed as possible, reference the specific paragraphs, pages or documents from your prior submissions where this information is discussed, and be sure to tell UNHCR when you are providing new information, and explain why you did not provide that information before.

Section 4: Why you meet the definition of a refugee under the Convention

In a section called "I am a Refugee under the Convention" write about why you qualify as a refugee under the Convention. You must meet the following criteria to qualify as a refugee under the Convention:

1. You must be outside the country you are from;
2. You must be unable or unwilling to return to the country you are from;
3. Because you have a well-founded fear:
   a. You must be afraid; and
   b. There must be objective evidence from your country (e.g. newspaper articles, NGO reports, UN reports) that shows you have a good reason to be afraid;
4. That if you return to your country, you will be persecuted (e.g. there is a threat to your life, freedom, or other fundamental human rights);
5. Based on one or more of the following reasons:
   a. Your race;
   b. Your religion;
   c. Your nationality;
   d. Your political opinion; or
   e. Your membership in a particular social group (this could be your family or persons with similar backgrounds, habits or social status, often with a characteristic which is innate, unchangeable or fundamental).

You do not need to repeat all of the facts that you included in your initial RSD statement or earlier in your appeal statement. Rather, you should summarize all of the facts that show that you meet this definition and highlight the new (or newly clarified) facts that show that you are a refugee. It is helpful to go through UNHCR criteria in order and state which facts support each of the five criteria.

Section 5: Documents

You should provide UNHCR with any new documents that support your appeal, along with any documents that you specifically reference in your appeal. List the names of each of these documents in a section called "Documents" at the end of your statement.

Section 6: Signature

Finally, sign your appeal statement. You can also thank UNHCR for considering your appeal and say that the information you have included is the truth.

BEFORE YOU GIVE YOUR APPEAL TO UNHCR

Before you give your appeal statement to UNHCR:

- Reread the appeal statement to make sure that you have included everything you wanted to include to help UNHCR understand why its initial decision was incorrect and why you meet the Convention definition of a refugee.
- Make sure that everything you have included is the truth and has not been exaggerated.
- Make sure your appeal statement is organized in a way that makes sense.
- Check whether anything in the appeal is different to what you have said in your statement or registration interview with UNHCR or any other information that you have given or told to UNHCR. If anything is different, explain why.
- Make sure you keep a copy of the appeal statement for yourself.

WHEN YOU GIVE YOUR APPEAL TO UNHCR

- Be sure to give your appeal to UNHCR within thirty (30) days of the date provided on the Appeal Application Form.
- If the documents that you have listed in your appeal statement have not previously been given to UNHCR, then also give UNHCR copies of these documents at the same time that you give the appeal statement to UNHCR. Do not give any original documents to UNHCR.

ANNEX 1: UNHCR RSD PROCESS

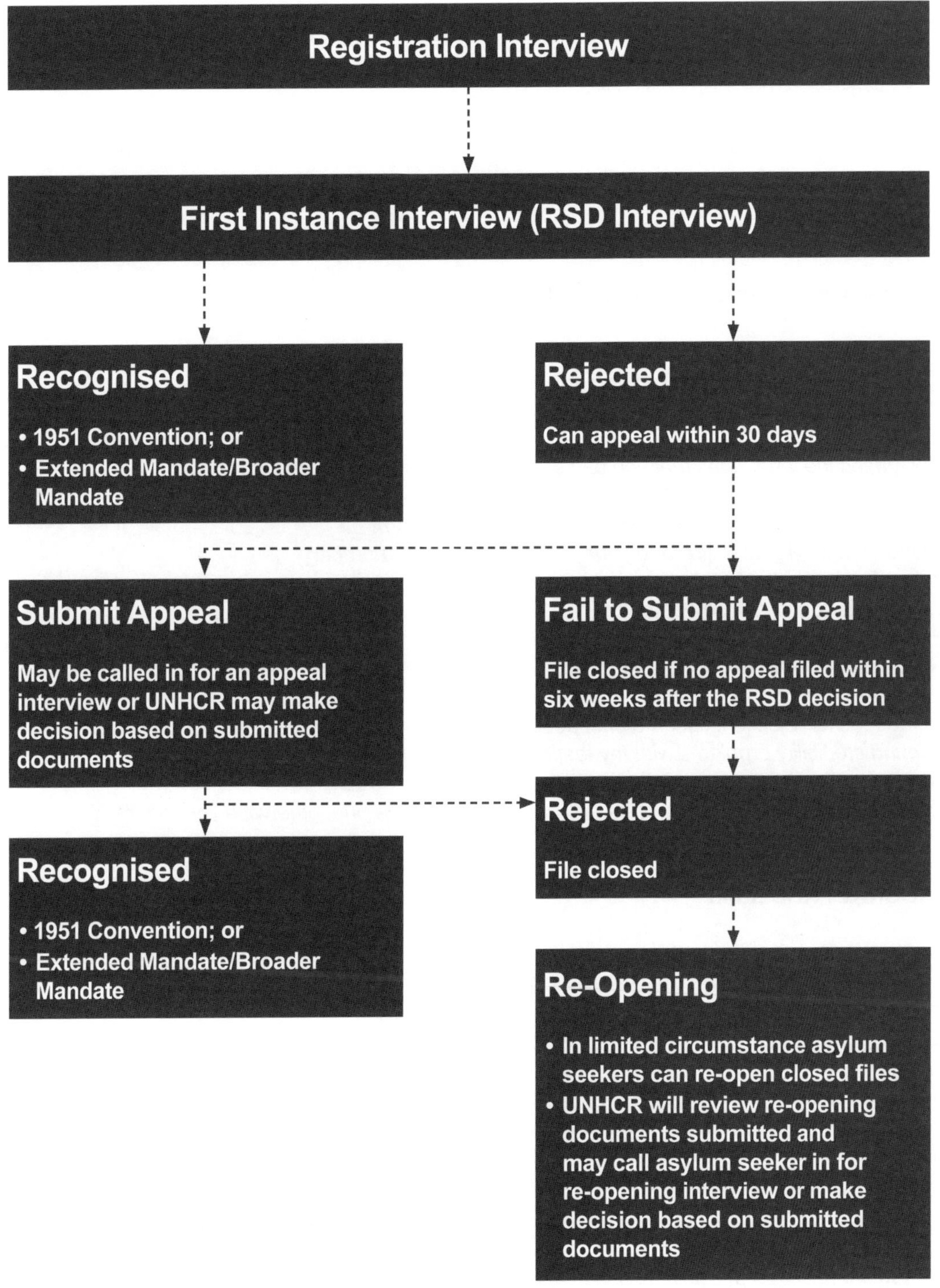

ANNEX 2: SAMPLE APPEAL STATEMENT

Your final statement could look something like the example below.

Date: [*insert the date that you're writing the letter*]

United Nations High Commissioner for Refugees

Attention: RSD Unit

Dear Sir/Madam,

My name is [*insert your name*] and this is my statement for my appeal with UNHCR.

NI Number: [*insert NI number*]
Gender: [*insert whether you're male or female*]
Nationality: [*insert your nationality*]
Ethnicity: [*insert your ethnicity*]
Languages: [*insert the languages that you can speak and understand fluently*]
Date of Birth: [*insert your date of birth*]
Place of Birth: [*insert the city and the country where you were born*]
Passport Country and Number: [*include your passport country ID number*]
Marital status: [*state whether you're married, single or widowed*]
Date arrived in this country: [*insert date*]
Date registered with UNHCR: [*insert date*]
Date of RSD interview with UNHCR: [*insert date*]
Date of notification of UNHCR decision: [*insert date*]
UNHCR's reasons for rejection: [*insert a brief description of the Rejection Reasons, for example "UNHCR found credibility problems with my testimony," or "UNHCR found that the harm I fear does not amount to persecution under the Convention"*]
Current contact information: [*insert your mobile number if you have one, otherwise your address*]

1. PROCEDURAL PROBLEMS

[*Set out any breaches of procedural fairness that the UNHCR committed during your interview, and explain why you think this affected the UNHCR's decision*]

2. REJECTION REASONS

2.1. [*Set out each of the Notification rejection reasons in separate headings; under each heading, give all of the reasons that you believe UNHCR should reconsider its decision, including whether UNHCR considered all of the evidence, there is new evidence that UNHCR should consider, or there were procedural problems during your RSD interview(s).*]

2.2. [*If you have new evidence, explain what this is and why this was not included previously; if you presented evidence that UNHCR did not properly consider, set out what the evidence is, your reasons for believing this evidence was not properly considered, and cross-refer to any earlier statements rejected because you did not give enough detailed information to support your claim; provide any additional information you have; focus on the specific areas where UNHCR has said it does not have sufficient information; put facts in chronological order whenever possible.*]

2.3. If you were rejected for credibility reasons, explain any inconsistencies in your prior evidence; provide as many objective facts as possible; focus on the specific areas that UNHCR points out in the Notification; put facts in chronological order whenever possible.]

2.4. [*If you were rejected because the harm that you fear is not "persecution" under the Convention, explain why the harm you fear falls into one of the categories listed above; explain why you fear that you will be persecuted if you return home.*]

2.5. [*If you were rejected because UNHCR believes that authorities in your country can protect you, explain why that is not the case; provide details about any attempts you (or others such as your family or neighbours) made to get help from the authorities.*]

2.6. [*If you were rejected because UNHCR believes that you can live in another part of your country, explain why you cannot live in that other part of the country; focus on both why you have a fear of persecution in this other place and why moving there would be a hardship.*]

3. I AM A REFUGEE UNDER THE 1951 CONVENTION

[*Set out how the you satisfy the Convention refugee definition; deal with each aspect of the definition under separate headings.*]

4. CONCLUSION

[*Conclude by asking UNHCR to recognise you as a refugee under the Convention.*]

5. DOCUMENTS

[*List any new documents that you are providing for the UNHCR.*]

All the information that I have included in this statement is true. Thank you for considering my application for refugee status.

[*Sign your name here*] ___________________________________

[*Print your name here*] ___________________________________

Appendix O – Self-Help Kit Re-opening Statements

Self-Help Kit

How to apply to re-open your UNHCR refugee status file

December 2009

Self-Help Kit
How to apply to re-open your UNHCR refugee status file

Table of Contents

WHEN DOES UNHCR CLOSE YOUR FILE?

The purpose of the UNHCR's Refugee Status Determination ("RSD") process is to determine whether you meet the definition of a refugee under the 1951 Convention relating to the Status of Refugees ("the Convention").[74] You must convince UNHCR that you meet each of the requirements of the Convention definition of a refugee. UNHCR can only help you if you meet the definition of a refugee – the fact that you might be suffering for other reasons is not relevant to UNHCR.

UNHCR uses any statements you have given them, your RSD interview(s), and information from your home country to decide whether you meet the Convention definition of a refugee.

If UNHCR rejects your RSD application, you have the right to appeal. If you have appealed and your appeal has been rejected by UNHCR, then UNHCR will close your file.[75] UNHCR will also close your file if:

- you told UNHCR that you were withdrawing your RSD application, or
- you did not attend your RSD interview with UNHCR and you did not contact UNHCR within 6 weeks of the scheduled interview date, or
- you did not appeal after UNHCR rejected your RSD application.

If UNHCR closes your file, then UNHCR will no longer consider you to be an asylum seeker and will not give you an asylum seeker certificate.

In certain circumstances (explained below), you can apply to re-open your file.

The purpose of the re-opening process is for UNHCR to make sure that it has understood and considered all of the facts of your case and correctly applied the Convention refugee definition to the facts of your case. Just like in your initial RSD application, the question in your re-opening application is whether you meet the Convention definition of a refugee.

If UNHCR decides to re-open your file, UNHCR may call you in for another interview to help them decide whether you are a refugee. However, UNHCR may decide not to re-open your file without interviewing you.

WHAT IS THE PURPOSE OF THIS SELF-HELP KIT?

To ask UNHCR to re-open your file, you need to write a statement requesting UNHCR to re-open your file and explain why you are asking for this.

This Self Help Kit will help you decide whether you should apply to re-open your file, and to understand what information you should include in your re-opening statement.

WHEN SHOULD YOU APPLY TO RE-OPEN YOUR FILE?

1. <u>If UNHCR never made a decision about your case</u>

If you withdrew your RSD claim before UNHCR made a decision about your refugee status, and you ask UNHCR to re-open your file, then UNHCR will re-open it.

If you did not attend your RSD interview and did not contact UNHCR within 6 weeks of your interview date, UNHCR will usually re-open your file <u>unless</u> you missed several interviews without a good explanation and UNHCR considers that you are not being honest.

In either of these circumstances, you should write a letter to UNHCR asking UNHCR to re-open your file, and explain why you are asking for this. You should also explain why you missed an interview and did not contact UNHCR.

You can get a copy of our RSD self-help kit that explains how to write your statement to UNHCR, to make sure that you have told UNHCR all relevant information about your case.

2. If your RSD claim was rejected by UNHCR and you did not know that it had been rejected

If your RSD claim was rejected and you did not appeal because you were not notified of the decision or the deadline for appealing, then UNHCR will usually re-open your case.

In these circumstances, you should write a letter to UNHCR asking UNHCR to re-open your file, so that you can appeal, and explain that you were not notified of the decision or the deadline for appealing.

You can get a copy of our appeal self-help kit that explains how to write an appeal statement, to make sure that you have told UNHCR all relevant information for your appeal.

3. If your claim was rejected by UNHCR after your RSD interview or after your appeal

If:

- your RSD claim was rejected, you knew your claim was rejected, you knew about the deadline for appealing, but you did not appeal; or
- you appealed and UNHCR rejected your appeal, then

UNHCR will only re-open your RSD file if one of the following circumstances applies:

a. There is reliable new information of a significant change in your personal circumstances or the conditions in your home country that may substantially affect your eligibility for refugee status.

Examples of this might be:

- a new event has happened in your home country that shows you are at greater risk of persecution there
- something has happened to you in this country that puts you at greater risk of persecution in your home country

b. You have reliable, relevant and important new information which helps to establish that you meet the Convention refugee definition.

You need to explain to UNHCR why this information was not given to UNHCR earlier (eg because you only just found out about it, or you could not get the documents earlier).

c. There is serious reason to believe that UNHCR did not properly decide your RSD claim, and/or that UNHCR did not adequately consider the grounds on which you might be a refugee.

This means that UNHCR made a mistake when it rejected you, either because it did not understand properly what happened to you, or because it made a mistake when applying the Convention refugee definition to your case.

If you did not appeal against the rejection of your claim by UNHCR, you need to explain why you did not appeal.

This self-help kit does not deal with how to argue that UNHCR did not correctly apply the Convention definition of a refugee. However, the Convention refugee definition is explained below.

The rest of this self-help kit explains how to write a re-opening statement that deals with the other reasons to re-open your file, as outlined in paras (a) – (c) above.

Think carefully about whether you should apply to re-open your file

UNHCR will not change its decision if you have already presented all relevant information, UNHCR already understands the facts of your case, and UNHCR's application of the Convention refugee definition is clearly correct.

If UNHCR has already rejected your claim, you should think carefully about whether you want to ask UNHCR to re-open your case, since:

- it will probably take UNHCR a long time to consider your application
- only a small number of re-opening applications are successful, and usually these are cases where there is important new information, and
- while you are waiting for UNHCR to decide whether to re-open your file and re-consider your case, you will not usually have an asylum seeker certificate, and without this, you will probably not be able to obtain any assistance from refugee NGOs.

WHAT IS THE PURPOSE OF YOUR RE-OPENING STATEMENT?

The aim of your re-opening statement is to convince UNHCR that it made a mistake and that you meet the Convention definition of a refugee. This is the only issue that is relevant to UNHCR.

Do not repeat information that you have already given UNHCR, since they will have this on your file.

If you did not appeal when UNHCR rejected your RSD application, then you should get a copy of our appeal self-help kit, and follow the guidelines in that self-help kit as to how to write an appeal statement addressing the UNHCR's rejection reasons, as well as following the guidelines below.

Your re-opening statement should:

- provide any new information or clarify information that UNHCR did not understand or has not previously considered; and
- explain how all your information shows that you meet the Convention definition of a refugee.

THINGS TO REMEMBER WHEN WRITING YOUR RE-OPENING STATEMENT

When you write your re-opening statement, remember that:

- Your statement should be in your own words and must only include information that is true and that is not exaggerated.
- If you can write in your own language then you should write your statement.
- If you cannot write in your own language, make sure that the person who writes the statement for you only includes information that you have told them to include.
- Do not let anyone tell you what to include in your statement or let anyone add anything to your statement that you disagree with or that is untrue.
- You should try to keep your statement to less than 6 pages if it is not in English, because if it is longer it will take UNHCR more time to translate it.
- If there are things you don't remember, do not make something up. It is fine to say that you don't remember.
- If there is something you are not sure about then you should say something like, "I believe that ..." or "I think that ..." but don't say, "I know that ...". Also explain why you are not sure.
- Your statement should be consistent with all information that you have previously told or given to UNHCR. If you plan to include information in your statement that is not consistent with information that you have previously told or given to UNHCR, then explain the inconsistencies in your statement.

WHAT TO INCLUDE IN YOUR RE-OPENING STATEMENT

One way you can organize your re-opening statement is explained here.[76] Remember, this is only an example and you don't have to organize your re-opening statement this way. What is important is that you explain why UNHCR should reconsider its decision and why you meet the Convention definition of a refugee.

Section 1: UNHCR address and personal information

Write the date, UNHCR's address and address the letter to UNHCR. Then, introduce yourself and say that you are applying to UNHCR to re-open your RSD file.

Write your UNHCR ID number, gender, nationality, ethnicity, date of birth, place of birth, the languages that you speak fluently, passport country and number (if you have one), marital status, the date you registered with UNHCR, the date(s) of your first instance interview(s) with UNHCR, the date of notification of UNHCR's reasons for rejection, the date of UNHCR's rejection of your appeal (if any) and your current contact information.

Section 2: New information

Explain any new important events that have occurred since UNHCR rejected your claim, that help to show that you are at risk of persecution if you go back to your home country. These events may involve you personally, your family, friends or colleagues, or the conditions in your home country.

For example, something may have happened to you in this country that puts you at greater risk of persecution in your home country, or something may have happened in your home country to your family members or other people with similar profiles to you, which show that you would be at risk of persecution if you went home. Alternatively, something may have happened politically or with the security situation in your home country that now places you at greater risk of persecution.

If you have recently found out about any other relevant information that you have not previously told UNHCR, explain what this information is and why you were not able to give UNHCR this information before (eg because you only just found out about it, or you could not get the documents earlier).

If you have remembered other relevant information that you did not tell UNHCR before, then set out this information and explain why you did not previously mention it (eg because you did not realise that it was relevant, or because you forgot about it).

Make sure that you put information in chronological order and be as detailed as you can, including things like names, dates, times, places, what people said or did, or why they said or did it.

Do not repeat information that you have already told UNHCR (although you can refer back to your previous statements or documents already given to UNHCR).

Section 3: How UNHCR made a mistake in its decision-making

If you think that UNHCR made a mistake either because it did not properly understand what happened to you or because it did not properly apply the refugee definition to your case, then explain why in this section.

If you think that UNHCR did not properly understand the information that you provided, then explain what mistakes you think UNHCR made and why it made those mistakes (eg there were problems with interpretation, you did not have the opportunity to present relevant evidence or the interviewer did not treat you fairly), and clarify the information that you provided.

If you think that UNHCR did not properly apply the refugee definition to your case, then explain why (see section 4 below).

If you did not appeal after UNHCR rejected your claim, explain why you did not appeal.

Section 4: Why you meet the definition of a refugee under the Convention

In a section called "I am a Refugee under the Convention" write about why you qualify as a refugee under the Convention. You must meet the following criteria to qualify as a refugee under the Convention:

1. You must be outside the country you are from;
2. You must be unable or unwilling to return to the country you are from;
3. Because you have a well-founded fear:
   a. You must really be afraid; and
   b. There must be objective evidence from your country (e.g. newspaper articles, NGO reports, UN reports) that shows you have a good reason to be afraid;
4. You must be afraid that if you return to your country, you will be persecuted (for example, you will be killed, raped, tortured or arbitrarily detained or that there are other threats to your fundamental human rights);
5. Your persecution must be for one or more of the following reasons:
   a. Your race;
   b. Your religion;
   c. Your nationality;
   d. Your political opinion; or
   e. Your membership of a particular social group (this could be your family or persons with similar backgrounds, habits or social status, often with a characteristic which is innate, unchangeable or fundamental).

You do not need to repeat all of the facts that you included in your initial RSD statement or your appeal statement. Rather, you should summarize the facts that show that you meet this definition and highlight the new (or newly clarified) facts that show that you are a refugee.

Ask UNHCR to recognise you as a refugee under its mandate.

Section 5: Documents

You should provide UNHCR with copies of any new documents that support your re-opening. List the names and dates of each of these documents in a section called "Documents" at the end of your statement.

Section 6: Signature

Thank UNHCR for considering your application and say that the information you have included is the truth. Finally, sign your statement and print your name under your signature.

BEFORE YOU GIVE YOUR RE-OPENING STATEMENT TO UNHCR

Before you give your re-opening statement to UNHCR:

- Re-read the statement to make sure that you have included everything you wanted to include to help UNHCR understand why you meet the Convention definition of a refugee.
- Make sure that everything you have included is the truth and has not been exaggerated.
- Make sure your statement is organized chronologically, and in a way that makes sense.
- Check whether anything in the statement is different to what you have said in your earlier statements or any other information that you have given to or told UNHCR. If anything is different, explain why.
- Make sure you keep a copy of the re-opening statement for yourself.

WHEN YOU GIVE YOUR RE-OPENING STATEMENT TO UNHCR

If you have listed new documents in your statement, then also give UNHCR <u>copies</u> of these documents. <u>Do not</u> give any original documents to UNHCR.

AFTER YOU GIVE YOUR RE-OPENING STATEMENT TO UNHCR

Sometimes UNHCR will not tell you if your re-opening application has been refused.

If you have not heard from UNHCR 6 months after giving them your re-opening statement, ring UNHCR to ask whether they have made a decision yet.

ANNEX 1: UNHCR RSD PROCESS

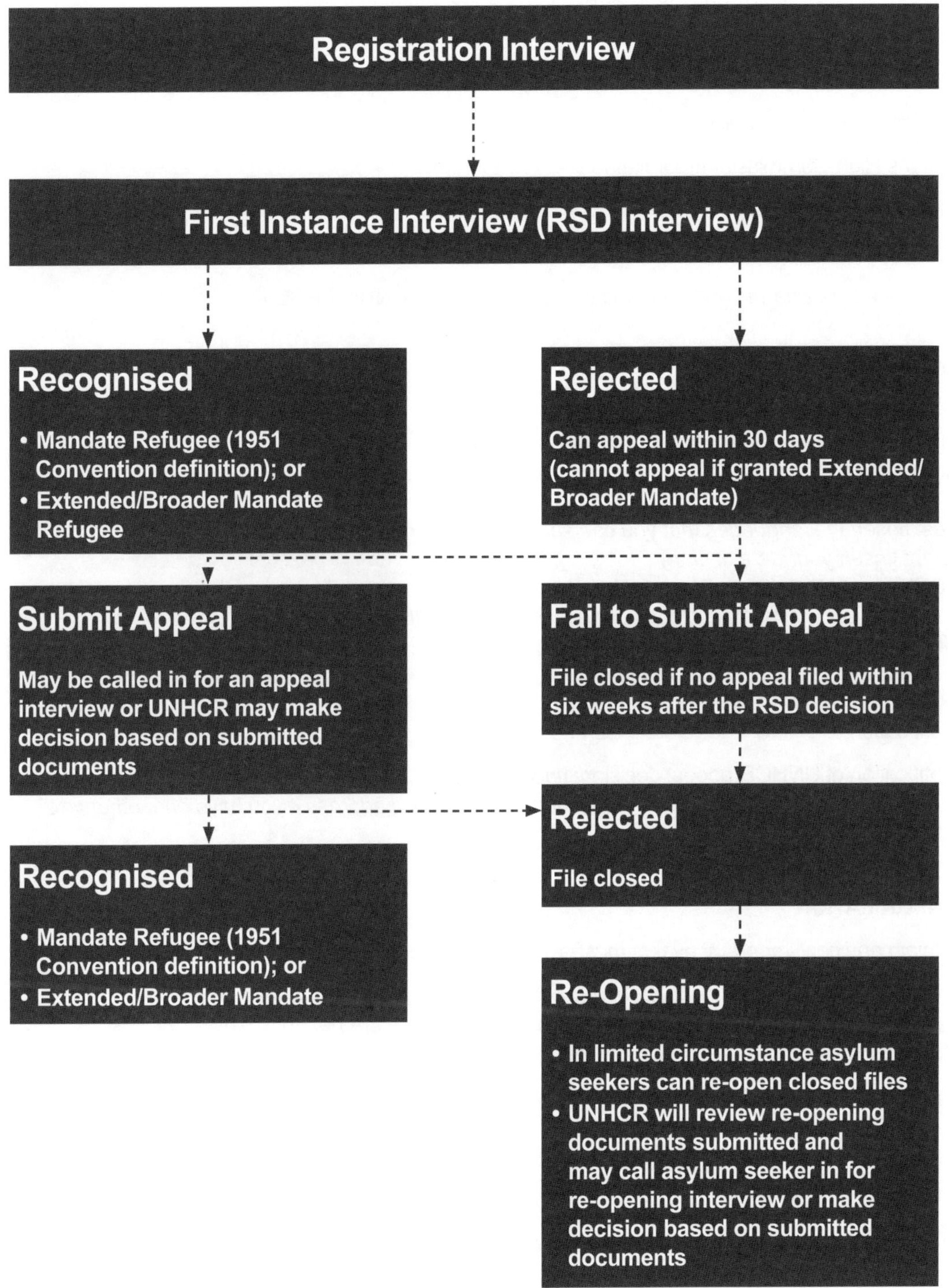

ANNEX 2: SAMPLE RE-OPENING STATEMENT

Your final re-opening statement could look something like the example below.

Date: [*insert the date that you are writing the letter*]

United Nations High Commissioner for Refugees

Attention: RSD Unit

Dear Sir/Madam,

My name is [*insert your name*] and I am applying to re-open my UNHCR RSD file.

1. PERSONAL INFORMATION

UNHCR ID Number: [*insert UNHCR ID number*]
Gender: [*insert whether you are male or female*]
Nationality: [*insert your nationality*]
Ethnicity: [*insert your ethnicity*]
Languages: [*insert the languages that you can speak and understand fluently*]
Date of Birth: [*insert your date of birth*]
Place of Birth: [*insert the city and the country where you were born*]
Passport Country and Number: [*include your passport country ID number*]
Marital status: [*state whether you're married, single or widowed*]
Date registered with UNHCR: [*insert date*]
Date of RSD interview with UNHCR: [*insert date*]
Date of notification of UNHCR decision: [*insert date*]

Date of notification of UNHCR appeal decision: [*insert date*]
Current contact information: [*insert your mobile number and email address if you have one, otherwise your address*]

2. NEW INFORMATION

2.1. [Explain any new important events that have occurred since UNHCR rejected your claim.]

2.2. [If you have recently found out about any other relevant information that you have not previously told UNHCR, explain what this information is and why you were not able to give UNHCR this information before.]

2.3. [If you have remembered other relevant information that you did not tell UNHCR before, then set out this information and explain why you did not previously mention it.]

3. UNHCR MADE A MISTAKE

3.1. [(If applicable) explain why you think that UNHCR did not properly understand the information that you provided, and why it made those mistakes, and clarify the information that you provided.]

3.2. [(If applicable) explain why you think that UNHCR did not properly apply the refugee definition to your case.]

3.3. [If you did not appeal after UNHCR refused you refugee status, explain why not.]

4. I AM A REFUGEE UNDER THE 1951 CONVENTION

[*Set out a summary of the facts that show how you meet the Convention refugee definition*]

[*Ask UNHCR to recognise you as a refugee under its mandate.*]

5. DOCUMENTS

[*List any new documents that you are providing for the UNHCR.*]

All the information that I have included in this statement is true. Thank you for considering my application to re-open my refugee status file.

[*Sign your name here*]

____

[*Print your name here*]

Appendix P – Sample First Instance Declaration[77]

FIRST INSTANCE DECLARATION

Name:	Morad
UNHCR File No:	02CO2953
Nationality:	Iranian
Religion:	Christian
Passport Number:	CJ073194561
Date of Birth:	06/09/1990
Place of Birth:	Tehran
Marital Status:	Single
Languages:	English and Farsi
Date of arrival:	06/08/2012
Date of registration with UNHCR:	12/08/2012
Date of first instance interview with UNHCR:	28/08/2012
Current telephone:	**07686 1995689**

My name is Morad and I am 22 years old. I was born and grew up in Tehran, which is the capital of Iran.

Until I was forced to leave Tehran I lived with my parents and my three brothers and two sisters. My family are all strict followers of Islam.

During my university studies, a friend of mine told me that he had converted to Christianity. He started to talk to me about Jesus.

As a result I began to attend a secret meeting of Christians that was held every week on my university campus. I began to believe in Jesus Christ and chose to become a Christian. That happened two years ago.

I was fearful about how my parents would react to my conversion along with other family members if I told them I had become a Christian so I kept it a secret from my family.

Two years after becoming a Christian I was arrested by the State Police and imprisoned in Evin Prison, which is in Tehran. The reason for my arrest and imprisonment was that I was accused of converting from Islam to Christianity.

I was held in solitary confinement for twelve days. During this time I was repeatedly beaten by the prison guards. The beatings took the form of punches that were inflicted to my stomach area, my lower back and my head by two or three prison guards. This happened on three separate occasions.

Whilst the prison guards were beating me they would say this was a punishment because I had insulted Islam by following Jesus and that I should be killed. During my imprisonment I was interrogated by the Savak secret police of Iran. They asked me questions about how many Christians I knew, how I was approached, did I support America and Israel against Iran and many other questions. They accused me of being a spy for America and Israel.

After twelve days in solitary confinement at Evin Prison I was brought before a District Judge who ordered me to recant my faith. He said that if I did not follow his order I would be executed.

I said in court: "I am now a follower of Jesus and I will not turn my back on Jesus." I was taken back to prison.

Three days later I was released from prison without any explanation. I was not given any paperwork but the secret police officials who had interrogated me told me that they would follow my every move.

Upon my release from Evin prison I went to my family home, where I discovered that all my belongings had been destroyed by my father. When I tried to talk to my father he threatened me by telling me that I had 30 minutes to leave the house otherwise he, my brothers and my uncle would kill me because I had brought shame on the family since I had converted from Islam to Christianity.

I really believed that my father would act on this threat so I was forced to leave my home even though I love my family a great deal. I realised I would not be safe anywhere in Iran.

My Christian friends told me that Christians are a target for arrest and imprisonment everywhere in Iran. I also know that the Iranian authorities punish Muslims who convert to any other religion and individuals have been executed or imprisoned for life because they have converted or been accused of converting. This happens not under the Iranian criminal code but under sharia law.

Real risk of persecution if returned to Iran

As a result of my arrest, imprisonment and the threats to kill me that I received, I realised that I had to leave Iran because I would always be subject to a real risk of death, torture and imprisonment because of the decision I had taken to change my religion.

There are two sources of this risk: first the Iranian authorities, including the Police and the Secret Police, and secondly my fellow Iranian citizens, many of whom act to show their obedience to Islam and also to the Iranian regime.

I realised wherever I lived in Iran I was at risk. In the last year over 300 Christians have been arrested and detained. These arrests have happened in the six major cities in Iran.

It was upon this realisation that I took a hard decision to leave my home country and to seek asylum in a country where I know I can freely practise and express my religious beliefs without risk of death, imprisonment or physical harm.

Everything contained in this statement is true and accurate:

....

[Name]

This statement was interpreted with the help of:

....

[Interpreter's name]

Date:

Appendix Q – Sample Closing Statement

Closing Statement for NAME (FILE NUMBER)

Mr. XXX should be granted refugee status under the 1951 Convention Regarding the Status of Refugees on the basis of his Fur ethnicity and imputed political opinion as a suspected Sudanese Liberation Movement rebel. Additionally, Mr. XXX should be recognized under the 1969 OAU Convention as an asylum-seeker fleeing Darfur.

1951 Convention: Ethnicity – (Fur); Imputed Political Opinion – (Suspected SLM rebel)

Mr. XXX's village of Bidinga was attacked and burned by the Janjaweed and government forces in 2004 during a sweep of violent attacks across the region. The inhabitants of Bidinga, all of whom were from the Fur tribe, were forced to flee en masse during the attack. Mr. XXX fled with his mother, stepsister and other villagers from Bidinga and made his way to Hamidia IDP camp.

While in Hamidia, Mr. XXX spoke out about the atrocities committed in Darfur and the resulting difficulties faced by internally displaced populations in the region. In an interview with Radio Dabanga in 2009, Mr. XXX criticized the Sudanese government's decision to expel aid agencies from Darfur and spoke about the consequences of this decision for those still living in IDP camps in the region. As a result of this interview, Mr. XXX was arrested during an attack on Hamidia camp a few months later. The Sudanese security forces who arrested him had known him during his secondary school days in nearby Zalingei and, recognizing his voice in the broadcast, decided to arrest, detain and torture him for speaking out.

Radio Dabanga, a Dutch-based independent radio station reporting on Darfur is recognized internationally as "the only media outlet routinely providing uncensored information" about the region.[78] In October of 2010, the radio station's Khartoum office was raided and 13 people were arrested and held incommunicado in unknown locations.[79] In a statement about the arrests, a Sudanese intelligence official accused Radio Dabanga of "working against Sudan, focused on inciting hatred among the people and aborting the peace process."[80]

According to Human Rights Watch, these arrests are "part of a wider pattern of stifling expression about ongoing human rights abuses in Darfur."[81] In light of this trend of crackdowns on activists, journalists and those who speak out about what is happening in Darfur, it is not surprising that Mr. XXX was arrested and tortured as punishment for telling Radio Dabanga about the abuses faced by his friends and neighbors in Hamidia IDP camp.

During his detention by Sudanese officials, Mr. XXX was repeatedly accused of rebel activity and associating with the Sudanese Liberation Movement. His release from detention was based upon the condition that he would provide information to the government about rebels in Hamidia camp. Mr. XXX did not follow this condition and, after evading arrest by security officials who came to look for him in the camp, he fled to Khartoum and then to Egypt.

Mr. XXX believes that as a young Fur man who has been accused of rebel activity, he is particularly at risk in Sudan. In its position on asylum-seekers from Darfur, the UNHCR confirms that young men of fighting age who return to Sudan are "regularly singled out for detention and interrogation."[82] Given his previous arrest and detention, along with the fact that he disobeyed the conditions he signed upon his release, Mr. XXX faces serious risk of harm if he returns to his country.

1969 OAU Convention: Events seriously disturbing the public order

The ongoing conflicts in Darfur have resulted in a death toll exceeding 300,000 according to recent UN figures[83] and has led to the displacement of over two million people[84]. The situation in the region continues to be unstable as the reports suggest the government continues to attack and burn civilian areas while raping women, killing innocent civilians and enlsiting child soldiers.[85]

Mr. XXX **should be granted refugee status under both the 1951 Convention Regarding the Status of Refugees and the 1969 OAU Convention and given the protection of your office**.

Appendix R – Checklist for RSD Interview Procedures

Procedure			Comment
Was Legal representative allowed in RSD interview. (4.3.3) [Make sure to provide written consent to act as legal representative]	☐ Yes	☐ No	
Was third party (other than Legal representative or associated UNHCR staff) allowed to attend RSD interview? (4.3.4)	☐ Yes	☐ No	
OPENING RSD INTERVIEW			
Did UNHCR officer introduce him/ herself and every other party by name and functional title? (4.3.4)	☐ Yes	☐ No	
Did UNHCR provide a translator of the same gender for the RSD interview? (4.3.4)	☐ Yes	☐ No	
Did the UNHCR interviewer confirm that the Applicant and translator understood each other and that the Applicant was comfortable with? (4.3.4)	☐ Yes	☐ No	
Did UNHCR Interviewer inform Applicant that any problems with quality or accuracy of interpretation should be addressed as the problems arise? (4.3.4)	☐ Yes	☐ No	
Did UNHCR Interviewer explain the purpose of the RSD interview and how it would proceed? (4.3.4)	☐ Yes	☐ No	
Did the UNHCR Interviewer explain the purpose of the notes that would be taken by him/her? (4.3.4)	☐ Yes	☐ No	
Did the UNHCR Interviewer explain that the Applicant has a right to ask for a break during the interview? (4.3.4)	☐ Yes	☐ No	
Was Applicant informed of his/her right to confidentiality of information from interview? (4.3.4)	☐ Yes	☐ No	

Was Applicant informed that if he/she didn't know an answer to a question, or clarification was needed, that he/she should tell UNHCR interviewer? (4.3.4)	☐ Yes	☐ No	
Did UNHCR Interviewer ask whether Applicant felt physically and psychologically fit to move forward with RSD interview? (4.3.4)	☐ Yes	☐ No	
Was Applicant given opportunity to ask questions or make preliminary remarks before the interview started? (4.3.4)	☐ Yes	☐ No	
QUESTIONING THE APPLICANT			
Did UNHCR Interviewer use primarily open-ended questions? (For instance, "how did you feel? Instead of "did you feel frightened?) (4.3.6)	☐ Yes	☐ No	
Did UNHCR Interviewer request a description of events in chronological order? (4.3.6)	☐ Yes	☐ No	
During the interview, did UNHCR Interviewer identify any inconsistencies between Applicant's account and other evidence/accounts? (4.3.6)	☐ Yes	☐ No	
Did UNHCR Interviewer allow an opportunity for Applicant to clarify incomplete or contradictory facts or statements? (4.3.6)	☐ Yes	☐ No	
RECORDING INTERVIEW			
Was the interview transcript recorded by computer during the RSD interview?	☐ Yes	☐ No	
If not recorded by computer, was the transcript hand-written?	☐ Yes	☐ No	

Appendix S – Sample Template for Appeal

APPEAL OF FIRST INSTANCE DECISION IN APPLICATION FOR REFUGEE STATUS

Applicant:	
Refugee Applicant ID #:	
Case Status:	
Country of Origin:	
Passport/ID Number:	
Religion:	
Marital Status:	
Language(s):	
Gender:	
Date of Birth:	

Attention: Minister of Foreign Relations

Dear Minister:

On ____________________ (date), my application for refugee status was denied on the following basis: ________________________________ (reason application denied).

I respectfully request that you reconsider the negative decision made in the first instance of my application for refugee status. I am a refugee under the definition provided in the Refugee Convention of 1951. In this letter I will provide the reasons for which my appeal should be accepted.

1. Summary of the request

2. Reasons for the appeal

In the Submission, all Legal Advisors are to only address the grounds of appeal (i.e., new information, procedural errors, errors of law, etc.) that apply to each case. That is, there is no need to address every ground if it is not relevant or does not apply. Significant COI may be referred to and/or attached to the Submission.

- **New Information/Information not previously disclosed**: New information that is relevant to the claim and was not available at the first instance/appeal interview or if it was available reasons why it was not provided before, e.g. incidents that have occurred after the applicant fled their country.

- **Procedural Errors:** Procedural problems that arose during the first instance/appeal interview, such as problems with the interpreter. The Legal Advisor should critically assess any procedural error claim as OdR keeps a complete transcript of their interviews and we are aware that some applicants have been instructed by others to fabricate such claims.

- **Conditions in COI:** Brief description of applicant's situation in COI and any security/medical concerns/issues etc.

- **Any *Sur Place* Claims:** Individuals who become refugees after leaving their country of origin due to a change in circumstances in/out of their country.

- **Errors of Law**: There may be cases where we should write legal submissions in relation to an Error of Law. These include (but are not limited to) the following circumstances:

  - The legal issues in the claim are complex;
  - The claim arises under multiple grounds of the Convention;
  - The applicant is extremely vulnerable and may be eligible for resettlement;
  - We received full reasons for rejection;
  - There are known credibility issues that need to be addressed and;
  - The claim is unusual/unique.

3. Conditions in the host country

4. Support documents

5. Conclusion

Respectfully submitted,

Name	Signature	Date

Appendix T – Sample Appellate Legal Brief

Name:

UNHCR:

DATE: 28 JULY 2011

LEGAL BRIEF

Summary of claim

1. Mr. __________ appeals his rejection for refugee status under the 1951 Refugee Convention (Convention).

2. In brief, Mr.________ is a national of Iran who has converted to Christianity. As a Christian convert, and one who wishes to educate others about his conversion, Mr. __________ faces a significantly increased risk of being persecuted on the basis of religion. In addition, he has participated in political anti-regime demonstrations, heightening the risk of persecutory conduct.

3. The reason for Mr. __________'s rejection is contained in part of the Notification of Reasons for Decision, stating:

> **"...the Office has determined that there is not a reasonable possibility that you would experience harm upon return to your country since there is no indication that the authorities have become aware of your identity. From your statement, you clearly state that there was no attempt by the authorities to pursue you after your escape. Based on this, it is further determined that the chance that you would face harms on the account of your religion does not amount to the level of reasonable possibility."**

4. Accordingly, credibility is not at issue. The single issue to determine is whether, based on the profile of the appellant, there is a reasonable possibility of serious harm related to a Convention reason.

5. The "well-founded fear of being persecuted" aspect of the Convention is a future looking test. It is also a very low threshold. The fact that the authorities have not taken direct action in the past is an indicator of what will occur in the future, but is not determinative. It is merely one factor in the assessment.

6. In looking at the cumulative profile of the appellant, and taking account of the future conduct of the appellant to proselytize, there is a reasonable chance that he will face persecutory conduct on the basis of his religious conversion.

7. In addition, the country of origin information and jurisprudence support a conclusion that Christian converts face a well-founded fear of being persecuted. In light of this information, the decision should

be overturned or, at the least, he should be invited for an appeal interview to determine the extent of his future conduct upon return to Iran.

Profile of the Appellant

8. Before proceeding it is important to determine the profile of the appellant. According to the Notification of Reasons for Decision credibility is not at issue making the profile easier to determine.

9. Therefore, and from the evidence of the appellant, his profile includes the following factors:

   a. Born in Tehran in _______ in a Muslim family and brought up in that faith.

   b. Interested in Christianity but unable to access much about the religion in Iran.

   c. Went to the United Kingdom in ______ and was baptized on __________.

   d. He applied for asylum in the UK, but left before his appeal had been determined due to poverty.

   e. Upon return to Iran he attempted to proselytize out of commitment to his conversion and because this is central to his belief.

   f. He engaged in anti-regime protest at the time of the "Green Revolution". He was arrested, but managed to escape before being detained. The police did not take down his details.

   g. He came to ________ in May 2010 and applied for refugee status.

   h. On return to Iran, his evidence is that he will continue to attempt to proselytize, to promote Christianity, and to express his opinion regarding the "truth" as to religious belief.

10. The cumulative profile of the appellant, therefore, is one who has converted, proselytized, and who will continue to proselytize.

Threshold – "well-founded fear"

11. It is clear that the "well-founded fear" test is future looking. This was helpfully summarized by the English Court of Appeal in Katrinak v. Secretary of State for the Home Department, [2001] EWCA Civ 832 where the Court stated:

    > **"The definition of refugee … looks to the future. The past is only relevant in as much as it is one of the evidential factors which is often, but not always, relevant to consider when deciding whether the claimant has a well-founded fear that he will be persecuted in the future if he returns to the country of his nationality."**

12. The question, then, is what is the likelihood of persecutory conduct.

13. This threshold question has been considered in all jurisdictions. The Notification of Reasons for Decision refers to the "reasonable possibility" test which draws on language taken from the United States Supreme Court decision of I.N.S. v. Cardoza-Fonseca (1987) 467 U.s. 407.

14. Other helpful formations of the test can be found from the following jurisdictions:

    a. R. v. S.S.H.D., ex parte Sivakumaran, [1988] 1 All E.R. 193 (U.K. House of Lords): "reasonable degree of likelihood."

    b. Adjei v M.E.I., [1989] 57 DLR 4th 153 (Canada Federal Court of Appeal): "serious possibility."

c. Chan v. M.I.E.A., (1989) 63 ALR 561 (High Court of Australia): "real chance."

15. The upshot of all this is that the test is actually a low threshold. It is not required to prove the likelihood of persecutory conduct beyond reasonable doubt, as in criminal proceedings. Nor, is it even required to be proved on the balance of probabilities or preponderance of the evidence – that the persecutory conduct is more likely than not.

16. Indeed, this makes sense given the protection purpose of the Convention. It also means that in refusing a claim, the decision-maker should not engage in pure speculation around the possibility (or not) of future serious harm. There must be tangible evidence to displace the likelihood of such conduct,

17. In rejecting this case, it was considered fundamental to Mr. ________'s application that he was not subsequently pursued following his escape. In the first place, this assumes that no attempts were made by the authorities. In the absence of evidence indicating this, this is close to speculative (although clearly relevant). That may be explained by a number of factors, including whether the authorities had his correct details or not.

18. The Handbook (at paragraph 196) speaks of the joint burden between the asylum seeker and the decision-maker to determine the likelihood of persecutory harm in order to prevent refoulement. It states:

> **"...[W]hile the burden of proof in principle rests on the applicant, the duty to ascertain and evaluate all the relevant facts is shared between the applicant and the examiner. Indeed, in some cases, it may be for the examiner to use all the means at his disposal to produce the necessary evidence in support of his application."**

19. In that context, then, and in the knowledge that the threshold is low, let us review the country of origin information relevant to this case.

Country of origin information

20. As Appendix "A" to this brief we have provided a comprehensive collection of the relevant country of origin information with highlighted sections that are particularly relevant. We will not canvas that information here, but will attempt to summarize the key pieces of information relevant to Mr. _________'s case.

21. The United Kingdom: Home Office, Operational Guidance Note – Iran, 15 March 2011, v6, (available at: http://www.unhcr.org/refworld/docid/4d7f54a42.html) summarises the situation in Iran:

> **"3.8.7 The Iranian government does not respect the right of Muslim citizens to change or renounce their religion. Proselytising of Muslims by non-Muslims is illegal. The government charged members of religious minorities and others with crimes such as 'confronting the regime' and apostasy and followed the same trial procedures as in cases of threats to national security. According to Article 513 of the Iranian Penal Code, anyone who insults the Holy Islam or the Prophet or any Imam, as well as the Prophet Mohammed's daughter, will be punished by death if the insult is so radical so as to amount to the rejection of the Prophet, Saabolnabi (equivalent to apostasy). Otherwise, the offender would be sentenced to between one and five years imprisonment."**

22. The country of origin information indicates that anti-Christian and anti-apostate activity has increased since the appellant left Iran. The United Kingdom: Home Office, Country of Origin Information Report – Iran, 28 June 2011, (available at: http://www.unhcr.org/refworld/docid/4e26ead814.html) quotes another report in illustrating this point:

> **"19.42 The USCIRF Report 2011 stated that:**
>
> **During the reporting period [1 April 2010 to 31 March 2011], the number of incidents of Iranian authorities raiding church services, harassing and threatening church members, and arresting, convicting, and imprisoning worshippers and church leaders has increased significantly."**

23. This reporting period is particularly relevant – it covers the period of Mr. _________'s stay in Thailand. The increased persecutory actions by the Iranian state only compounds Mr. _______'s initial reasons for flight.

24. The same source (that is, the UK Home Office) expands on this increased risk in the preceding paragraph:

> **19.41 An article dated 10 January 2011 by the Hudson Institute's Center for Religious Freedom, reported developments since the end of 2010:**
>
> **"After arresting Iranian Christian pastor Behrouz Sadegh-Khanjani and passing a death sentence for apostasy on Yousef Nadarkhani, pastor of the Full Gospel Church of Iran congregation in Rasht, the Iranian government is now conducting a massive roundup of Christians, often converts from Islam and including evangelical and ethnic Armenian Christians. As is becoming common in the region, it started its latest repression on a Christian holy day, Christmas.**
>
> **"Beginning on December 26 [2010], security forces raided Christian homes in Tehran and elsewhere, abused and handcuffed their occupants, and dragged 25 people off to prison and interrogation. Amongst those taken were married couples, at least two of whom were forced to leave babies behind. Police raided another dozen houses but the occupants were not at home – the homes were ransacked, looted, and sealed, and their occupants ordered to turn themselves in to the authorities.**
>
> **"Since these Christmas attacks, the regime has arrested at least another 30 or 40 Christians in a series of ongoing raids – some sources say as many as 601. Some of those detained have been released, but most have been detained without charge or explanation, and without access to lawyers or family. Middle East Concern reports that on January 4 [2011], the governor general of Tehran Province, Morteza Tamadon, acknowledged that Christians had been arrested because of their 'corrupting' influence and warned that there would be further arrests.**
>
> **"This is the largest targeted Iranian violence against Christians since the government assassination campaign**

against Protestant leaders in the mid-1990s, and perhaps since the earliest years of the revolution." [96a]

25. There is clearly a very compelling climate of fear for Christians, and particularly converts, currently in Iran.

26. The Operational Guidance Note cited above (at paragraph 21) at paragraph 3.8.4 goes to the heart of this claim:

> **"As long as the private sphere remains private and Islamic rules and values are not visibly challenged or violated, the Iranian authorities will not normally intervene in citizens' private sphere. All non-Muslim minorities generally maintain a low profile in public as regards religious affiliation. As long as they follow the rules, minorities can practise their religion without being in the authorities' spotlight because this constitutes lawful and socially acceptable behaviour."**

27. This a key point. Mr. __________ will not maintain a discrete profile. He feels compelled [see his Farsi (first instance) and Appeal Testimonies] to speak out about Christianity. It is central to his belief. In doing so, he is directly challenging Islamic values in the eyes of the authorities.

28. This is compounded by a further distinction, that of being an "ethnic" or "non-ethnic Christian". This is explained at paragraph 19.36 of the 28 June 2011 UK Operational Guidance Note (cited above at 21):

> **"Generally speaking, there are two groups of Christians in Iran, who may be classified as ethnic and 'non-ethnic'. Ethnic Christians include the Armenians, Assyrians and Chaldeans. Many of them are followers of the Orthodox Church, but some are also Catholics or Protestants. 'Non-ethnic' Christians are mostly followers of the Protestant and Evangelical churches and many are converts from Islam.**
>
> **"The recognition of Christianity as one of the three non-Islamic religions accepted by the Constitution has given a safe margin to the ethnic Christians only. 'Non-ethnic' Christians, however, have faced great pressure because, unlike the 'ethnic' Christians, they are involved in proselytising."**

29. Clearly, Mr. __________ fits within the "non-ethnic" description.

30. According to sources listed in the Appendix, apostasy in Iran is punishable by law (see: United Kingdom: Foreign and Commonwealth Office, Human Rights and Democracy: The 2010 Foreign & Commonwealth Office Report; US Department of State 2010 Country Report on Human Rights Practices, Iran; for interpretation of apostasy in a political, historical context see UK Home Office Country of Origin Information Report, August 2010).

31. Sources are unclear, however, as far as the legal basis for punishment is concerned. While sources state that apostasy is punishable by death by law (e.g.: US State Department 2010 Report), some say that apostasy is not currently regulated directly in the current Iranian penal code.

32. In 2009 the Iranian Government proposed to remove articles that refer to death penalty for apostasy. However, sources are either silent on the progress of the proposal or say there is no information concerning the status of the articles in question.

33. It seems that the (death) penalty applied in case of apostasy does not necessarily derive from actual articles in the Iranian penal code but more from the interpretation of Islam. (e.g.: United Kingdom: Home Office, Country Of Origin Information Report – Iran, 31 August 2010, p120).

34. Sources were uncertain regarding apostasy charges and the resulting penalty. There were no reported cases of apostasy between July 2009 and June 2010 according to the United States Department of State, 2010 Report on International Religious Freedom.

35. On the other hand, the UK Home Office Country of Origin Information Report 2010 says that the lack of information on apostasy prosecution might be explained by the use of ancillary offences. As we have seen above, a large number of Christians have recently been arrested and detained – with some not heard of since arrest – so there is clearly a policy and practice of targeting this group.

36. In sum, then, the country of origin shows that the Christian convert, the "non-ethnic" Christian, who does not act discretely and attempts to proselytize, may come to the attention of the authorities and will suffer persecutory conduct as a result. This may include arrest, detention, torture, and on-going monitoring following the release to restrict freedom of expression.

Future conduct of the appellant

37. The appellant's evidence is that he will continue to proselytize. As outlined in both his Farsi and Appeal Testimonies, he sees it as an obligation to spread the "truth" of his religion. In particular, he views it as a requirement to engage with those Muslims who are conservative in their beliefs. This will expose them to a different perspective and, the appellant argues, some form of enlightenment that Mr. ________ feels that he himself has undergone.

38. Given that evidence, he will not act discretely upon return. Since his departure from Iran, the situation has become far more critical for Christian converts (see paragraph 24 above). The possibility of being informed upon to the authorities is clearly real. It rises to the level of well-foundedness precisely because of the appellant's belligerence in spreading, as he phrases it, the "truth".

39. Nor should the Convention require him to act discretely. By way of analogy, the UK Supreme Court in HJ (Iran) & HT (Cameroon) v SSHD [2010] UKSC 31 at paragraph 54 makes this point by quoting Simon Brown LI in Ahmed (Iftikhar)v Secretary of State for the Home Department [2000] INLR1, at page 7:

> **"It is one thing to say … that it may well be reasonable to require asylum seekers to refrain from certain political or even religious activities to avoid persecution on return. It is quite another thing to say that, if in fact it appears that the asylum seeker on return would not refrain from such activities – if, in other words, it is established that he would in fact act unreasonably – he is not entitled to refugee status."**

40. The point, bluntly, is that Mr. ___________ will not refrain from proselytizing.

41. An additional area of concern is what may happen to him on return at the border. As he explains in his Appeal Testimony [at paragraph 10], he was earlier given a restriction in his passport. This may alert him to further questioning on return and rise the level of suspicion regarding his stay in Thailand.

42. Remembering that the threshold is low for well-foundedness, and given the country of origin information, it is a reasonable possibility that Mr.________ will continue to proselytize and will come to the attention of the authorities – it may not happen immediately, but his chances of detection are highlighted by his actions in seeking to speak openly about his religion.

Reason for rejection

43. Let us repeat the stated reason for rejection:

> **"...the Office has determined that there is not a reasonable possibility that you would experience harm upon return to your country since there is no indication that the authorities have become aware of your identity. From your statement, you clearly state that there was no attempt by the authorities to pursue you after your escape. Based on this, it is further determined that the chance that would face harms on the account of your religion does not amount to the level of reasonable possibility."**

44. Given this finding, it is important to review the circumstances surrounding the escape, although this is explained in the Farsi and Appeal Testimonies, and remembering that the escape was held to be credible.

45. First, he was not arrested due to his religious conversion. He was taking part in protests that were incredibly chaotic where a large number of people were being arrested and taken away.

46. Second, he managed to escape through pure luck and was able to quickly mingle with the crowd. It is not surprising, given the chaos at the time, that the police did not pursue him with doggedness.

47. Third, the police never asked his details. In this case, they were unable to follow up. Again, in the context of the protests and the large number of arrests, it is not surprising that the authorities did not further pursue him.

48. Fourth, had he not escaped, there is a strong possibility that the authorities would have then become aware of his conversion through interrogation. The escape was a piece of incredibly good fortune.

49. In these circumstances, then, the reason for rejection does not properly address the key aspects of Mr. _________'s claim. The real assessment should be around his future conduct and whether what he asserts in his testimonies is credible.

Conclusion

50. Given his conversion and commitment to proselytizing, Mr. __________ cannot return to Iran. He requires the protection of the Convention. At the very least, he should be invited for an Appeal Interview to determine the credibility of his future conduct and whether that conduct brings him within the scope of Convention.

APPENDIX U – CHRISTIANS IN IRAN COUNTRY OF ORIGIN INFORMATION

1 GENERAL SITUATION

Human Rights Watch, *World Report 2011 - Iran,* 24 January 2011, available at:
http://www.unhcr.org/refworld/docid/4d3e801e0.html

"Iranian laws continue to discriminate against religious minorities, including Sunni Muslims, in employment and education. Sunni Muslims, about 10 percent of the population, cannot construct mosques in major cities. In 2010, security forces detained several members of Iran's largest Sufi sect, the Nematollahi Gonabadi order, and attacked their houses of worship. They similarly targeted converts to Christianity for questioning and arrest."

United States Department of State, *2010 Country Reports on Human Rights Practices - Iran,* 8 April 2011, available at:
http://www.unhcr.org/refworld/docid/4da56dbd2.html

> **"The constitution provides for the establishment of political parties, professional associations, Islamic religious groups, and organizations for recognized religious minorities, as long as such groups do not violate the principles of 'freedom, sovereignty, and national unity' or question Islam as the basis of the Islamic Republic. The government limited freedom of association in practice through threats, intimidation, imposing arbitrary requirements on organizations, and arresting group leaders and members."**

United Kingdom: Home Office, *Operational Guidance Note – Iran,* 15 March 2011, v6, available at:
http://www.unhcr.org/refworld/docid/4d7f54a42.html

3.8.7 The Iranian government does not respect the right of Muslim citizens to change or renounce their religion. Proselytising of Muslims by non-Muslims is illegal. The government charged members of religious minorities and others with crimes such as 'confronting the regime' and apostasy and followed the same trial procedures as in cases of threats to national security. According to Article 513 of the Iranian Penal Code, anyone who insults the Holy Islam or the Prophet or any Imam, as well as the Prophet Mohammed's daughter, will be punished by death if the insult is so radical so as to amount to rejection of the Prophet, Saabolnabi (equivalent to apostasy). Otherwise, the offender would be sentenced to between one and five years imprisonment.

3.8.8 A letter from the Foreign and Commonwealth Office (FCO) dated 30 April 2010 stated that: "Under Iran's strict interpretation of Islam, anyone converting to another religion could face the death penalty or at least life imprisonment" and that "the number of Christians and Christian converts arrested or detained in Iran has increased significantly over the last two years. 38 Associated Press recently reported that Iran had arrested about 70 Christians since Christmas in a crackdown that has targeted grass-roots Christian groups Iran describes as "hard-liners" who pose a threat to the Islamic state.

2 CHRISTIANS

United Kingdom: Home Office, *Operational Guidance Note – Iran,* 15 March 2011, v6, available at: http://www.unhcr.org/refworld/docid/4d7f54a42.html

3.8 Christians/Christian converts

3.8.1 Some applicants may make an asylum and/or human rights claim based on ill-treatment amounting to persecution at the hands of the state due to their conversion to Christianity or actively seeking to convert others (proselytising).

3.8.2 ***Treatment.*** The Iranian Constitution explicitly declares Islam to be the state religion but contains two important provisions concerning religious minorities. Article 13 states that Zoroastrian, Jewish and Christian Iranians are the only recognised religious minorities who are free to perform their religious rites and ceremonies, within the limits of the law, and to act according to their own principles in matters of personal affairs and religious education. Article 14 also provides protection for non-Muslims, provided they refrain from conspiracy or activity against Islam and the Islamic Republic of Iran.

3.8.3 However in practice all religious minorities experience varying degrees of officially sanctioned discrimination, particularly in employment, education, and housing. Since the 1979 Iranian revolution, members of minority religious communities have fled Iran in significant numbers for fear of persecution.

3.8.4 Iranian religious tradition differentiates between offences committed in the public domain and that which takes place within the confines of privacy. Offences that are in violation of Islam and that are committed in the public domain must be punished, while what takes place in the private sphere, and is thereby concealed, is tolerated to a greater extent. This can include, for example, drinking of alcohol, prohibited sexual relations, use of illegal films, books, music and religious practice. Irrespective of their ethnic and religious background, very many Iranians in practice live two lives, one in the public domain and another in private. As long as the private sphere remains private and Islamic rules and values are not visibly challenged or violated, the Iranian authorities will not normally intervene in citizens' private sphere. All non-Muslim minorities generally maintain a low profile in public as regards religious affiliation. As long as they follow rules, minorities can practise their religion without being in the authorities' spotlight because this constitutes lawful and socially acceptable behaviour.

3.8.5 After Ahmadinejad was elected president in 2005, the situation for everyone who can be suspected of being in opposition to the regime has deteriorated. Religious minorities have also experienced a general worsening of the political climate and government actions continue to support elements of society who create a threatening atmosphere for some religious minorities.

Endnotes

1. Convention Relating to the Status of Refugees, opened for signature 28 July 1951, 189 U.N.T.S. 137 [Convention]. http://www2.ohchr.org/english/law/pdf/refugees.pdf (accessed 15 August 2011). For a survey of earlier refugee accords, see James C. Hathaway, *The Law of Refugee Status*. London: Butterworths, 1991, pp. 2-6. For a concise review of the development of refugee law, see Laura Barnett, "Global Governance and the Evolution of International Refugee Regime", *14 Int'l J. Refugee L.* 238. http://oppenheimer.mcgill.ca/IMG/pdf/Barnett.pdf (accessed 17 August 2011).

2. Protocol Relating to the Status of Refugees, opened for signature 31 January 1967, 19 U.S.T. 6223, T.I.A.S. No. 6577, 606 U.N.T.S. 267 [Protocol]. http://www2.ohchr.org/english/law/pdf/protocolrefugees.pdf (accessed 15 August 2011). For description of the fundamental concepts of the Convention, see also Erika Feller, "International refugee protection 50 years on: The protection challenges of the past, present and future", *IRRC*, Vol. 83, No. 843 (September 2001), pp. 582-583. ("The 1951 Convention is a landmark in the setting of standards for the treatment of refugees… These include the following: that refugees should not be returned to persecution or the threat of persecution [the principle of non-refoulement]; that protection must be extended to all refugees without discrimination; that the problems of refugees is social and humanitarian in nature and, therefore, should not become a cause of tension between states; that since the grant of asylum may place unduly heavy burdens on certain countries, a satisfactory solution of the problem of refugees can be achieved only through international cooperation; that persons escaping persecution cannot be expected always to leave their country and enter another country in a regular manner and, accordingly, should not be penalized for having entered into or being illegally in the country where they seek asylum; that given the very serious consequences that the expulsion of refugees may have, this should only be resorted to in exceptional circumstances to protect national security or public order and; that cooperation by States with the High Commissioner for Refugees is essential if the effective coordination of measures taken to deal with the problem of refugees is to be ensured.")

3. International Commission of Jurists, *Migration and International Human Rights Law – Practitioners Guide No. 6*. Geneva: International Commission of Jurists, 2011, p. 47, citing Guy S. Goodwin-Gil, *The Refugee in International Law*. Oxford: Oxford University Press, 2nd Edition, 1998, p. 175; Alice Edwards, "Human Rights, Refugees and The Right 'To Enjoy' Asylum", *17 Int'l J. Refugee L.* 293 (2005), p. 299. http://oppenheimer.mcgill.ca/IMG/pdf/Migration_ and_International_Human_Rights_Law.pdf (accessed 15 August 2011).

4. United Nations Convention on the Status of Refugees, http://www2.ohchr.org/english/law/pdf/refugees.pdf (accessed 15 August 2011). See also generally UNHCR, "Advisory Opinion by the UNHCR on the Interpretation of the Refugee Definition", 22 December 2004. http://www.unhcr.org/refworld/pdfid/4551c0374.pdf (accessed 16 August 2011).

5. Asylum Access "Refugee Definition Flowchart".

6. See *UNHCR Compilation of Case Law on Refugee Protection*, UNHCR – Status Determination and Protection Information Section (SDPIS), March 2008.

7. UNHCR, *Handbook on Procedures and Criteria for Determining Refugee Status under the 1951 Convention and the 1967 Protocol relating to the Status of Refugees*. Geneva: UNHCR, 1992, para. 41 (accessed 16 August 2011).

8. International Commission of Jurists, *Migration and International Human Rights Law – Practitioners Guide No. 6*. Geneva: International Commission of Jurists, 2011, p. 49. See also UNHCR, *Handbook on Procedures and Criteria for Determining Refugee Status under the 1951 Convention and the 1967 Protocol relating to the Status of Refugees*. Geneva: UNHCR, 1992, paras 37-44. http://www.unhcr.org/3d58e13b4.html (accessed 16 August 2011). *Contra* James C. Hathaway and William S. Hicks, "Is There a Subjective Element in the Refugee Convention's Requirement of 'Well-Founded Fear'", *26 Mich. J. Int'l L.* 505 (the authors argue, contrary to most commentators, that

there is no subjective element in the well-founded fear standard). http://www.refugeecaselaw.org/documents/2005MJIL-SubjectiveElement.pdf (accessed 16 August 2011).

9. *Idem*, paras 42-50.

10. Al Najar v. Ashcroft, 257 F.3d 1262, 1289 (11th Cir. 2001).

11. 480 U.S. 421; 107 S.Ct. 1207; 94 L.Ed.2d 434; 55 U.S.L.W.4313, 9 March 1987 (US Supreme Court).

12. R v. Secretary of State for the Home Department, Ex parte Sivakumaran and Conjoined Appeals (UN High Commissioner for Refugees Intervening) [1988] AC 958, 16 December 1987 (UK House of Lords); *See also UNHCR Compilation of Case Law on Refugee Protection*, UNHCR – Status Determination and Protection Information Section (SDPIS), March 2008, 4.

13. International Commission of Jurists, *Migration and International Human Rights Law – Practitioners Guide No. 6*. Geneva: International Commission of Jurists, 2011, p. 49. See also UNHCR, *Handbook on Procedures and Criteria for Determining Refugee Status under the 1951 Convention and the 1967 Protocol relating to the Status of Refugees.* Geneva: UNHCR, 1992, paras 51-60 (accessed 16 August 2011).

14. UNHCR, *Handbook on Procedures and Criteria for Determining Refugee Status,* paras 51-52.

15. *UNHCR Compilation of Case Law on Refugee Protection*, UNHCR – Status Determination and Protection Information Section (SDPIS), March 2008, 4, quoting Korablina v. Immigration and Naturalization Services, No. 97-70361, 158 F.3d 1038, 23 October 1998.

16. Practitioners Guide, p. 50.

17. UNHCR, *Handbook on Procedures and Criteria for Determining Refugee Status under the 1951 Convention and the 1967 Protocol relating to the Status of Refugees.* Geneva: UNHCR, 1992, para 68 (accessed 16 August 2011).

18. FS (Iran – Christian Converts) CG [2004] UKIAT 00303; R v. SoS for the Home Department ex parte Kazmi [1994] Imm AR 94, QBD.

19. Kazemzadeh v. Holder, the Ninth Circuit.

20. Kassatkine v. Canada (Minister of Citizenship and Immigration) [1996] 65 A.C.W.S. (3d) 480.

21. *Idem.*

22. T. Jeremy Gunn, "The Complexity of Religion in Determining Refugee Status", Roundtable on Religion-Based Refugee Claims, United Nations High Commissioner for Refugees and Church World Service, 24 October 2002; UNHRC, "Guideline on International Protection: Religion-Based Refugee Claims under Article 1A(2) of the 1951 Convention and/or the 1967 Protocol relating to the Status of Refugees", 28 April 2004.

23. Volker Turk, "Guidelines on International Protection: Religion-Based Refugee Claims under Article 1A(2) of the 1951 Convention and/or the 1967 Protocol relating to the Status of Refugees HCR/GIP/04/06 28 April 2004" *16 Int'l J. Refugee L.* 500, 502 (2004).

24. *Idem.*

25. *Idem.*

26. Kantoni v. Gonzalez, 461 F.3d 894, 898 (7th Cir. 2006).

27. Bucar v. INS, 109 F.3d 399, 405 (7th Cir. 1997).

28. Practitioners Guide, p. 50.

29. *Idem.*

30. UNHCR, *Guidelines on International Protection No. 2: "Membership of a Particular Social Group" Within the Context of Article 1A(2) of the 1951 Convention and/or its 1967 Protocol Relating to the Status of Refugees*, 7 May 2002, HCR/GIP/02/02, para. 11-13. http://www.unhcr.org/refworld/docid/3d36f23f4.html (accessed 17 August 2011).

31. Practitioners Guide, p. 51.

32. Islam v. Secretary of State for the Home Department; R v. Immigration Appeal Tribunal and Another, Ex parte Shah (A.P.), Session 1998-1999, United Kingdom: House of Lords, 25 March 1999, 25, citing In re Acosta, 19 I. & N. Dec. 211, 232-34 (BIA 1985).

33. Attorney-General of Canada v. Ward, 103 D.H.R. (4th) 1, 22-34 (1993).

34. Guy S. Goodwin-Gil, *The Refugee in International Law.* Oxford: Oxford University Press, 2nd Edition, 1998.

35. James C. Hathaway, *The Law of Refugee Status.* London: Butterworths, 1991.

36. *Idem.*

37. UN High Commissioner for Refugees, *Handbook on Procedures and Criteria for Determining Refugee Status under the 1951 Convention and the 1967 Protocol relating to the Status of Refugees*, January 1992, para. 88. http://www.unhcr.org/refworld/docid/3ae6b3314.html (accessed 17 August 2011).

38. Maarouf v. Canada (Minister of Employment and Immigration) [1994] 1 F.C. 723, 13 December 1993 (Canada Federal Court).

39. Canada (Attorney General) v. Ward [1993] 2 S.C.R. 689, 30 June 1993 (Supreme Court of Canada).

40. Horvath v. Secretary of State for the Home Department [2000] INLR 15, 6 July 2000 (UK House of Lords).

41. Asylum Access, "RSD Interview: What to Expect".

42. Helsinki Citizens Assembly, "Information for People Applying for Refugee Status in Turkey", August 2007.

43. Asylum Access "Self-Help Kit – How to Appeal UNHCR's Rejection of Your Application for Refugee Status", April 2009.

44. Helsinki Citizens Assembly, "Information for People Applying for Refugee Status in Turkey", August 2007.

45. *Idem.*

46. *Idem.*

47. *Idem.*

48. Asylum Access, "Materials, Inter-Agency Referrals".

49. Asylum Access, "Materials, Opening and Closing Statements". https://sites.google.com/a/asylumaccess.org/refugee-rights-learning-materials/refugee-legal-aid-manual/basics-key-concepts-of-legal-services/rsd-interview-preparation/rsd-interview-representing-your-applicant/opening-and-closing-statements.

50. *Idem.*

51. *Idem.*

52. Asylum Access, "Materials, Transcribing the Interview". https://sites.google.com/a/asylumaccess.org/refugee-rights-learning-materials/refugee-legal-aid-manual/basics-key-concepts-of-legal-services/rsd-interview-preparation/rsd-interview-representing-your-applicant/transcribing-the-interview.

53. *Idem.*

54. *Idem.*

55. *Idem.*

56. *Idem.*

57. Asylum Access "Appealing a Negative Decision". https://sites.google.com/a/asylumaccess.org/refugee-rights-learning-materials/refugee-legal-aid-manual/basics-key-concepts-of-legal-services/appealing-a-negative-decision.

58. Evangelical Alliance PQ Public Affairs, "Altogether for Asylum Justice", July 2007.

59. Michael Kagan, "The Beleagured Gatekeeper: Protection Challenges Posed by UNHCR Refugee Status Determination", *18 Int'l J. Refugee L.* 1 (2006). See also RSD Watch, "UNHCR's RSD Policy – Quick Guide". http://rsdwatch.wordpress.com/unhcrs-rsd-policy-a-guide/.

60. *Idem.*

61. UNHCR's Department of International Protection Services Director, George Okoth-Obbo.

62. Michael Kagan, "The Beleagured Gatekeeper: Protection Challenges Posed by UNHCR Refugee Status Determination" *18 Int'l J. Refugee L.* 1 (2006). See also RSD Watch, "UNHCR's RSD Policy – Quick Guide". http://rsdwatch.wordpress.com/unhcrs-rsd-policy-a-guide/.

63. *Idem.*

64. *Idem.*

65. Note: There is also another definition of a refugee, normally referred to as the "extended mandate" or "broader mandate" definition.

66. Even if you meet all of the five criteria set out above, under certain circumstances, such as if you have committed a serious crime (in another country) for a non-political reason, you may not be recognized as a refugee.

67. Have a look at the full Sample Statement.

68. Your mobile number if you have one, otherwise your address.

69. See definition.

70. As of June 2008 you cannot appeal if UNHCR grants "extended mandate" or "broader mandate" status.

71. See RSD process chart at Annex 1.

72. This is the date you received the decision, which is the date on the "Appeal Application Form," not the date on the "Notification of Reasons for Decision".

73. See the Sample Statement at Annex 2.

74. See definition.

75. See RSD process chart at Annex 1 on page 9.

76. See the Sample Statement at Annex 2.

77. This example is fictitious, but it is typical of applications that are or might be made by Iranian Christian converts from Islam.

78. Washington Post, "In Radio Dabanga raid, Sudan targets last uncensored media outlet on the ground", 10 November 2010, available at: http://www.washingtonpost.com/wp-dyn/content/article/2010/11/10/AR2010111003727.html (accessed 24 May 2011).

79. *Idem.*

80. *Idem.*

81. Human Rights Watch, "Sudan: End Continuing Repression of Darfur Activists", 2 November 2010, available at: http://www.hrw.org/en/news/2010/11/02/sudan-end-continuing-repression-darfur-activists (accessed 25 May 2011).

82. UNHCR, *UNHCR's Position on Sudanese Asylum-Seekers From Darfur*, 10 February 2006, available at: http://www.unhcr.org/refworld/docid/43f5dea84.html (accessed 25 May 2011).

83. CNNWorld, "Darfur rebel group: Government-run airports could be targets", February 2011. http://articles.cnn.com/2011-02-22/world/sudan.darfur.warning_1_darfur-peace-agreement-minni-minnawi-sudanese-air-force?_s=PM:WORLD (accessed 23 October 2011).

84. Human Rights Watch, "Unfinished Business: Closing Gaps in the Selection of ICC Cases", September 2011, available at: http://www.hrw.org/node/101558/section/7 (accessed 17 October 2011).

85. "Human Rights Report: Sudan", US State Department, April 2011, available at http://www.state.gov/g/drl/rls/hrrpt/2010/af/154371.htm (accessed 23 October 2011).